The
Natural Blues
and
Country Western
Harmonica

by
Jon Gindick

Illustrated by Bruce Thompson

*Additional Art: Ralph Homan, Denise Y. Clark,
Mark Sherman, Curt Vig*

The Cross Harp Press
San Diego • Visalia • Los Angeles

Distributed throughout the world by Music Sales Corporation:
33 West 60th Street, New York 10023
78 Newman Street, London W1P 3LA
4-26-22 Jingumae, Shibuya-ku, Tokyo 150
27 Clarendon Street, Artarmon, Sydney NSW 2064
Kölner Strasse 199, D-5000, Cologne 90

Library of Congress Catalog Card Number: 77-83727

ISBN: 0-930948-01-7

Dedicated to frustrated musicians all over the world.

INTRODUCTION

Ten years ago I bought my first harmonica. It was an Echo Harp, one of those double-reeded beauties with a picture of the Swiss Alps on the box. The harp had a tinny, ringing sound, not unlike something you'd expect Julie Andrews to play in the movie, "Sound of Music." Just looking at the crazy thing made you want to yodel.

As hard as I tried and as much as I practiced, I could not get beyond the cowboy-polka sort of thing I had played the first few minutes I had my Echo Harp out of its beautiful box. The best I could manage to play was a few old melodies like "Oh Susannah!", "Old Black Joe," and "Do Da, Do Da!".

Finally a guitar player who could stand it no longer took me aside and politely demanded that I buy a small Marine Band harmonica. When I had done this, he showed me the well-kept secret of playing **cross harp**.

Suddenly it all clicked. The bad notes began to disappear and a bluesy, jazz-like feeling came into my music. For the first time I could play improvisationally. For the first time **I could boogie**.

This book is a primer on the rules, ideas and skills of cross harp. It is designed to keep you from floundering, as I did for so many years, in the beginning stages of harmonica playing. This book doesn't attempt to teach you to play exactly like John Mayall, Sonny Terry, Norton Buffalo, or Charlie McCoy, but it does explain the fundamental principles that the great harpists follow. And it will teach you to interpret and apply these principles by listing the specific key of the harmonica you need to accompany each song on almost a hundred widely-owned record albums.

The idea is for you to begin jamming with records the same day you buy this book. Sound impossible? Well, it isn't. Not when you know what key of harmonica you need, and what notes will always sound good with any chosen music.

The chapters called "Cross Harp," and "Advanced Cross Harp," and the Record Index at the back of the book provide exactly that information. The rest of the book is devoted to the problems of playing the harp — getting single notes, bending single notes, making that harp talk. There is also a section called "Beginning Accompaniment" in which the principles of tuning and keying are explained as simply as possible.

Like the harmonica, this book is small enough to carry in your pocket, and it is simple enough to be understood. May it serve you well.

GLOSSARY

Blow: Blowing into your harmonica.

Draw: Sucking on your harmonica.

Cross Harp: A method of playing blues and country accompaniment and solo work on the harmonica. Cross harp accents the draw notes.

Straight Harp: A method of playing melodies on the harmonica. Straight harp accents the blow notes.

Single Note: Playing one note at a time. The holes of your harmonica are numbered. Drawing on hole number one is referred to as 1 draw. Blowing on hole number one is called 1 blow. In the illustrations, 1 draw is abbreviated to the circled numeral ①. 1 blow is the uncircled numeral 1.

Tension: The feeling of anticipation that is characteristic of blues and country harmonica music. It is most easily accomplished by playing cross harp and accenting the draw notes.

Harmonizing Note: A single note that you can play at any time in a song, and know that it will fit. Also known as a Safe Note.

Wailing Note: A Harmonizing Note that creates tension.

Note of Resolution: A Harmonizing Note that resolves tension.

Steppingstone Note: A note that does not harmonize. It is used as a steppingstone between Wailing Notes (which create tension) and Notes of Resolution (which resolve tension).

Blues and Country Harmonica Music: Creating and resolving tension with good tone to a beat.

Harmonica Chord: Three or more Harmonizing Notes played at the same time.

Key: A musical term which identifies the starting and ending place in a song or chord pattern, as in the key of A, or the key of E flat.

Tuning: Adjusting the guitar and other instruments to the harmonica.

Bending: Twisting the sound of the single note. You can only bend the draw notes.

TABLE OF CONTENTS

☆ THE DREAM ☆

THE REALITY

PATIENCE

PERSISTENCE

MORE PERSISTENCE

THE REWARD

GETTING STARTED

BUYING A HARP

The types of harmonicas that are best for playing cross harp are two and a half inches long (the Vest Pocket Harp is smaller) and they cost around nine dollars. If any of the albums in the Record Index have songs you especially want to accompany, buy a harp in the key that is listed for that song — if not — then I suggest the key of C.

1. Marine Band: The classic blues harmonica. My favorite — but could that just be sentiment?
2. Golden Melody: Highly recommended, except you can't play harp and guitar at the same time with this model.
3. Blues Harp: Nice tone, but sometimes they go bad quickly.
4. Special 20: A new model. Possibly the best. I recommend it very highly.
5. Vest Pocket Harp: A small, high quality harmonica. Excellent for children and other small people.
6. Chromatic Harps: Too sophisticated for blues, but the best for melodies and jazz.

BE CAREFUL TO BUY THE HARMONICA
THAT IS RIGHT FOR YOU.

When you buy your harp, be sure to have the salesperson test each hole. There is a law which prohibits you from putting the harp in your mouth before you buy it. This is why most music stores provide the squeeze-box tester. Don't trust it! After you've bought the harp, check it out for yourself. As you gently blow and draw each hole, listen for ringing sounds from the reeds. If you hear them, ask for another harp.

If you do buy a defective harmonica, return it to the store. The store manager doesn't have to replace it, but if he's a good guy, he will. If he's not a good guy, return the harp to its manufacturer in a padded envelope. Since Hohner makes the only harmonicas worth buying, your manufacturer will be M. Hohner, Inc. Their address is on the box.

If you buy four or five harmonicas at the same time, ask for a discount. Call around town until you find one.

STRAIGHT HARP

Straight Harp is the style of harmonica that most beginners play by accident. The first time they put the harp in their mouth, they blow, and then they draw. Straight Harp is playing your harmonica with the accent on the blow.

Bob Dylan sometimes plays straight harp and so does Charlie McCoy. It's an old fashioned style of music — good for playing Stephen Foster melodies and accompanying some of the mellowest, unbluesy folk music. Unless you are a harmonica virtuoso, it is impossible to play straight harp with the kind of power that you need to play blues.

The best way to learn straight harp is to figure out simple melodies. There are many books on the music store shelves that sell unrealistically complicated harmonica notation for songs like "Tie a Yellow Ribbon 'Round the Old Oak Tree" and "Hey Jude." Not only are these not particularly good harp songs, but they are often carelessly set down, and difficult to figure out.

The best straight harp songs to start out on are the ones that come to you naturally, the ones you've known since childhood. I'm thinking of songs like "Old Folks at Home," "Oh Susannah," and "Turkey in the Straw." You can usually figure these songs out, or find books that notate them.

A few of my favorites are notated in the section called "Melodies."

CROSS HARP

Cross Harp is the style of harmonica that plays blues. With the exception of the notes you get when you play 3blow and 6blow, cross harp accents the draw notes. This is important because you can bend draw notes, changing their shape and feeling by changing the shape of your mouth and throat. The distinguishing sound of cross harp is one note, say 4draw, being played for a long time, bending, wailing, creating tension.

The cross harp style is not very good for playing melodies. What it does best is accompany songs, and play riffs, simple patterns of notes that express the bluesy feeling in a way no other instrument can.

To get the idea of how cross harp sounds you should listen to other harpists. Some of my favorites on records are Charlie McCoy, Paul Butterfield, John Mayall, Sonny Terry, John Sebastian and John Loudermilk. These men are explosive, creative harp players. They play both straight harp and cross harp and other kinds of harp too, but usually they play cross harp.

Their music is often far more advanced than the simple patterns and runs described in this book, but it is based on the fundamental principle of creating and resolving tension.

The tension is anticipation, a feeling that the music is headed somewhere. Resolution is the feeling of arrival. Listen to country and blues records and see if you can hear or feel this principle at work. All music is based on the principle of creating and resolving tension, but is most obvious in country and blues.

Cross harp is the harmonica style that most effectively creates and resolves tension. This book teaches cross harp.

FIRST KISS

Fresh from its protective wax paper, your harp is an un-tested thing. It has a playing edge untouched by human lips and reeds as yet unmoved by human breath.

Be gentle with your harp. Place it to your lips and blow softly. Then draw. Are you relaxed? Lie on the floor or on your bed and place the harp between your lightly clenched teeth. Put your hands to your sides. Inhale slowly, deeply. Then exhale. Your harmonica should sound like a church organ.

Open your mouth large enough to cover the first four holes. Then blow and draw and listen to your tones. Let yourself relax. Continue your in-and-out breathing. Make it soft, controlled and natural so that the sounds coming from your harmonica will be soft, controlled and natural.

16

YOUR HARP

Your blues harmonica has ten holes, and each hole is numbered. On holes one through six, blowing will produce a lower note than drawing. To go up your harmonica one note at a time, you blow and draw on the first hole, blow and draw on the second hole, blow and draw on the third hole, and continue to blow and draw up through the sixth hole.

To continue up your harp, reverse the process. Draw and blow on the seventh hole, draw and blow on the eighth, ninth, and tenth holes.

The notes above 6draw are not very practical for the beginning harp player. They are difficult to play and aren't often used in modern harp styles.

Holes one through six, on the other hand, are the meat and potatoes of simple blues.

PLAYING SINGLE NOTES

Playing the single note correctly is the most important skill in harp playing. Contrary to the instructions in other manuals, the best way for a beginner to play a single note is to pucker.

Your face should be relaxed, your lips soft and moist and pushed out away from your face. **Pressing your lips tightly on the harp is the worst thing you can do. The only pressure in your facial muscles should be in the corners of your lips and cheeks.**

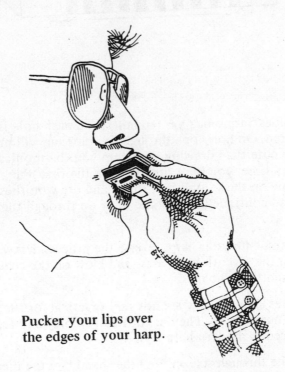

Pucker your lips over the edges of your harp.

It is the insides of your lips that touch the harp. They fit
on the top and bottom plates. The hole that your mouth
forms should be higher than it is wide — a vertical oval.

The muscle between your nostrils and upper lips should be
flaccid and almost perpendicular to your nose. Tightening
this muscle and tucking it under is a common and deadly
mistake.

Another common mistake is using your tongue to find the
note or guide the air. Although it is tempting to use your
tongue as a crutch, it belongs in the bottom of your mouth.
Keep it there!

Try to play a single note on 4draw. Your goal is to play it
without hiss, resistance, or that blurry chord sound that
you get when you include a little bit of a note other than
the one you are trying for.

BEGINNER'S BLUES RIFF

When you play beginning cross harp, the two most important notes are 4draw and 3blow. If you are tuned and keyed with a guitarist, record, or taped cassette, these notes will always work. When you play solo, 4draw and 3blow make up the framework of your blues riffs.

Play these notes with a taped cassette or record. Hold 4draw. Can you hear it harmonize? Slide the harp to 3blow. Does it merge with the music?

The Beginner's Blues Riff.

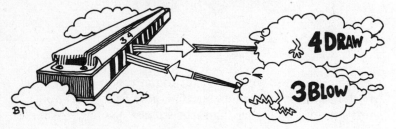

2draw and 3blow are the same notes. 3blow, however, is a little easier to play than 2draw. That is why the Beginner's Blues Riff is

④ ——————➤ 3

instead of

④ ——————➤ ②

 equals draw

BOOGIE!

The Beginner's Blues Riff might seem a little monotonous at first. You should realize, however, that any combination of notes would sound boring if it were played over and over, without feeling, like a doorbell or police siren.

There is music to be made on the Beginner's Blues Riff. If you can't find it in these two notes, you won't find it anywhere else.

Well, how do you boogie on two notes?

FIRST, you must be playing a clear single note.

SECOND, you must have control of your air.

THIRD, you must be able to punctuate your sounds.

Tonguing is the easiest and most effective way for a beginner to start making that harp talk.

Say ta ta ta ta. Did you notice how and where your tongue struck the roof of your mouth? Do it again. This time get a little fancier: tata tat. . tata tat. . . tata tat tat.

Your tongue is a wonderfully facile rhythm instrument. It is quick, clean, and virtually inexhaustible.

So, how do you boogie on the Beginner's Blues Riff?

One way is to pretend you are singing a song. Tongue each word in the song and even if you play only one note, your punctuation will sound like music instead of Morse Code.

SINGLE NOTE THERAPY

Can you feel tightness in your face? In your upper lip? In your jaw? Are you clenched up, ready to do battle with your blues harmonica?

The keys to a rich, clear tone are relaxation and a feeling of naturalness. These are difficult to accomplish when your harmonica is frustrating you. **You can't play a single note, so your mouth tightens up. Your mouth tightens up, so you can't play a single note.** (This is Gindick's Law). Pretty soon you are sucking tightlipped on your harp, and if you do manage to play a single note, it sounds hissy, cramped, and is impossible to bend.

Now that's no fun.

Loosen up your mouth with meditation and massage. A lot of the day's little frustrations end up in your mouth. Move them down to your foot or someplace. Then take yourself to a mirror, and calmly analyze what you are doing wrong.

Try to play a single note, pull the harp away, and examine the way you have formed your mouth. From a side view, your upper lip should be almost perpendicular to your nose, and shaped not unlike a pig's snout. From the front, your lips should push out to form a rough oval that is higher than it is wide.

This oval requires letting your jaw hang loose naturally, and pushing out your lips in much the same way as when speaking the **wh** in what.

Draw the air through your puckered lips so that it makes a hiss. Move your lips around so that the sound of the hiss changes. Think of your lips as a mouthpiece, and your body as a sound chamber.

Pushing your stomach out as you draw will change the sound of the hiss. So will changing the shape and size of the single note hole. The hole should be as large as possible so that your harp can fit on the insides of your lips. This takes a vertically long hole. All you have to do is drop your jaw a quarter of an inch and pucker in a natural way.

Feel the air strike the back of your throat. Change it so
that it makes a cold spot on the roof of your mouth. Move
the cold spot down into your throat, then down into your
belly. Move the cold spot back to your tonsils. Make it
cover as wide a spot as possible. Make the changes smooth
and powerful. This will prepare you for bending.

Try to be inventive as you move that cold spot around your
throat, body and head, and change the pitch of the hiss. Be
sure that your lips curve out and that you aren't pulling the
air through clenched teeth, or a tight, constricted mouthpiece.

Play your hiss of air with a song on the radio or record
player. Imagine a harp accompaniment, and play it with
your breath. Remember to make the long wailing hisses
on the draw. These are the notes you can bend. Be short
with your blows because in country and blues harp, they
are not as powerful as the draws.

Another thing to try without your harmonica is tonguing.
Whisper **ta ta ta ta** through your puckered lips. Feel your
tongue strike the roof. Feel how it stops your breath. Your
tongue is a wonderful rhythm instrument. Play it!

When you feel comfortable playing your breath through
oval lips in the mirror, try it with your harmonica. Avoid
any tendency to tighten up as soon as you put the harp in
your mouth.

Be patient with yourself.

BUT IT STILL SOUNDS LOUSY!

Playing a clean-sounding single note often takes awhile to learn. There are a lot of mistakes you can make. Most of these are rooted in the way you hold your mouth.

Should the air coming through your lips feel tight and constricted?

No. The most common reason for this problem is playing with a mouthpiece that is too small. It is also possible that you are putting too much pressure on the harp with your lips. Return to Single Note Therapy and learn to form an oval mouthpiece.

What if I'm always getting parts of other notes?

Then the hole in your mouthpiece is too wide. Drop your jaw and put a little bit of pressure in the corners of your lips as you pucker.

Why does my single note hiss?

Because you are not using the fleshy undersides of your lips to seal the harp. Your lips are tucked under instead of puckered. See the pictures. Note the line between the nostrils and the upper lip.

Why am I gasping for breath?

Take it easy. Breathe with your entire body, but control the airstream with your mouth and throat.

Why do I miss when I move the harp from one note to another?

Move the harmonica, not your head. Make your motions smooth and direct. Don't be in a hurry. When moving one hole as in the Beginner's Blues Riff, have your lower lip stick to the harp. Don't stop your breath between notes.

I can get a single note but it doesn't sound good with the taped cassette.

Your tape recorder may be slow or fast, making the music sound out of tune with the harp. Check your batteries or get your machine fixed. You might not be tuned or keyed correctly. Or, you might be flatting your single note, i.e., making it play lower than it is supposed to. Open up your nasal passages and relax your face. Draw the air through your harp so that you feel the airstream strike the roof of your mouth.

How come I lose my single note when I blow?

There is a tendency to lose control going from draw to blow. The blow triggers the collapse of your mouthpiece. Remember to use your mouth and throat to shape the stream of air that you push through your harmonica. Don't puff your cheeks. Try to make a smooth transition from draw to blow and blow to draw. Control the change with the air in the front of your mouth. Don't hyperventilate. It might help to cut the volume of air you are using in half.

BEGINNING ACCOMPANIMENT

WHY LEARN
TO ACCOMPANY?

Playing your harmonica with recorded music is one of the best ways to apply and understand the knowledge in this book. A note is just a sound, as indifferent as a car horn or a ringing telephone, until it becomes a part of a musical structure. In other words, the Beginner's Blues Riff sounds pretty funky until you use it to accompany your good buddy playing his guitar, or the stereo playing Willie Nelson, Linda Ronstadt, Sonny Boy Williamson, or another of your favorite musicians.

You will be amazed at the amount of music you can make playing the Beginner's Blues Riff and all of its variations. Threading only 4draw, or only 3blow, throughout an entire song will show you how the meaning and feeling of each note changes as the music it accompanies changes. You'll also discover that 4draw creates one kind of effect, that 3blow creates another, and that they both harmonize, i.e., they both sound good all the time.

The terms used in this book — "harmonize," "tension," "resolution of tension" — are ideas you will understand through feeling and experience instead of just reading about them. This is when you really start learning to play the harp. This is when the fun begins.

The first music you attempt to accompany, whether a taped cassette of a friend playing a two-chord progression on guitar, or a song from your favorite Eagle's album, should be slow and simple. If a harmonica already plays on the song you are trying to accompany, don't imitate it — not as a beginner, anyway. Start simply. Play at your own level. For a beginner, that level is the Beginner's Blues Riff and all of its variations.

To accompany records you must know what key harmonica to play with each song. The Record Index in the back of this book gives you this information for almost 100 records.

Simply find an album that I have listed and that you own, put it on your stereo, and play the key of harmonica noted for the song you wish to accompany. The trick is to find one song that works for you, and to explore it with your harmonica.

Bear in mind that some of these albums are harder to accompany than others. Beginners need steady, solid rhythm and simple chord patterns. I've found that country western, blues, rock, and folk albums are often the best music for the beginner to accompany.

YOUR HARP AND ITS KEY

A good harmonica player usually carries around a bag of harps so that he can accompany music that other people play. One harp might be in the key of G, another in the key of C, and another in B flat. What key of harp he chooses depends on the key of the music he is accompanying.

The harp player says to the guitar player, "Hey man, what key you playing this song in?"

The guitar player might answer, "Guess I'll play it in the key of G."

Then the harp player rummages through his bag of harps for the appropriate key of harmonica. The key that the harmonica is set in is etched on the right hand side of the harp's upper plate. Watch a harmonica player on a darkened stage search furiously through his harps for one set in a certain key. It is frustrating for him if he doesn't find it.

An F sharp is the highest harmonica you can buy. G is the lowest. The five most useful keys are A, C, D, F, G. Any songs and riffs that you learn in one key will work in any other key of harp too. It is more fun to have a few different keys if you are going to jam with people and records, but to start out you only need one.

THE TAPED CASSETTE

A beginning harp player needs simple, predictable guitar music with which he can play along. Two excellent 60 minute taped cassettes with two chord guitar music and examples of every riff in this book are available from The Cross Harp Press. But if you want to make your own tape, it's not difficult, and should be good experience.

You need a portable tape machine, a tape, and a guitarist. Machines are cheap and easily bought, borrowed or rented. You can buy a tape just about anywhere.

Guitar players are a little tougher to find, but not much. Your best bet is a friend who plays. If you don't have one, why not advertise and find somebody who lives nearby? Or if that doesn't work, take your recorder into a music store and buy a few minutes of a guitar instructor's time. You'll probably find a guitarist who is happy to oblige.

Ask your guitarist to play a two-chord progression in the key designated (see Tuning and Keying). No fancy stuff, please. Sevenths will give it that blues feel. The bass runs should be simple but strong so that you, the beginning harpist, can anticipate chord changes. Fancy riffs, rhythm changes, and key changes should be saved for another time. The recording should be about five minutes long.

Ask your guitarist to sing or hum. This will make it easier to hear and feel his chord changes.

31

TUNING AND KEYING

Before you can play with a guitarist, the guitar must be tuned to the harp. There are two E strings on a guitar, so E is a good note for him to tune to.

How do you find an E on your harmonica?

If you have an E harp, then blowing on the first and fourth holes produces E notes. If you have a D harp, you can blow on either the first or fourth hole and play a D.

If you want to play a scale, you must start from the fourth hole. On a C harp, 4blow is a C, 4draw a D, 5blow an E, 5draw an F, 6blow a G and so on.

The simplest way for a beginner to tune a guitar to a harp is to blow on the first hole, tell the guitar player what note it is, and let him tune to it.

Incidentally, on a C harp, you can play E notes on either 2blow or 5blow.

You also have to be sure that the guitar plays in the right key for the harp. This is one of the important tricks of playing cross harp.

Ask the guitarist what key he is playing. If he says A, then count up four from the A, including the A.

A B C D
1 2 3 4

And play a D harp.

If he says G, count up four, including the G.

G A B C
1 2 3 4

And play a C harp.

Guitar Key	Appropriate Harp
A	D
Bflat	Eflat
B	E
C	F
Dflat	Fsharp
D	G
Eflat	Aflat
E	A
F	Bflat
Fsharp	B
G	C
Aflat	Dflat

Now that's cross harp.

Straight harp, described more fully on page 86, is played on the same key of harmonica as the guitar, and the accent is on the blow instead of the draw.

A HARP PLAYER'S DREAM

This is your big night. You are auditioning for the Stallions, the country western and blues band that plays down at Annie's Tugboat on Friday, Saturday, and Wednesday nights. They say they need a harmonica player. Could it be you?

The band is setting up the equipment.

"What kind of mike do you use?" the bass player asks.

"Oh hell, I don't care," you say carelessly, wondering if you should bother to tell him that the only experience you've had with microphones was when you serenaded your ex-girlfriend over the telephone.

The lead guitar player sits on his amplifier and tunes his guitar. Incoherent notes leap from his fingers. You try to remember how to find an E note on a C harp in case he asks you. Finally you remember that 5 blow and 2 blow are both E's on your C harp. You play 2 blow. But by this time he is already tuned. He ignores you, and you turn away.

Playing softly to yourself, you think about how badly you want this job now that your unemployment insurance is ending. The thought of returning to your old job at the carwash is frightening. You thump the spit out of your harp with the palm of your hand and look around the room with a nervous smile. The music is starting up. The drummer hits his high hat. The bass player grabs his bass. They grin at each other and start to play. You panic. They haven't tuned with you, and you don't even know what key they're in. What harp should you use? Damn! You wish you had that book here with you.

The bass and the drums are laying down a solid crash-and-bang with their furious plucking and pounding. The lead guitar player leaps high into the air, and his flying fingers whip a fury of notes into the brew. His guitar whines, groans, exhalts and all of it right into your ear. You fight your way through a maze of wires and microphones to get over to him.

"What key are you playing in?" you shout.

He smiles at the dance of his fingers, lips curved into an expression of ecstasy and rapture. He doesn't hear you.

In angry desperation you turn to the bass player.

"What key?" you shout over the music.

"A," he mouths, and you whip out your A harp.

It sounds horrible. A loud, bleating honk right in the middle of the break. You begin to feel clammy now. That old feeling that you were born a loser and will always be a loser comes creeping back. Furtively, you look up from your hands. Did they hear that bad note?

Then you realize your mistake. You hadn't played cross harp. Key of A, huh? You count up four from the A – A, B, C, D – take your D harp from your gunstrap harmonica belt, and try again.

Puckering your lips over the fourth hole of the harmonica you carefully suck, and you listen to how the single note you are playing merges with the band. They aren't paying much attention to you and for this you are grateful. Already you can see yourself scrubbing windshields in your rubber suit. Suddenly you realize that the 4draw you are playing sounds pretty good.

36

You hold this note. It threads through the music and some-how it never makes a mistake. You begin to tongue it. Just steady little flicks of your tongue against the roof of your mouth — tat tat tatta tat tat — and voila! You're another John Mayall. You swell with pride and joy.

You had no idea it was so easy.

Then you realize that it isn't pride and joy that's making you swell. You've been drawing for thirty seconds and you're about to explode.

On the slimmest of chances you slide the harmonica to the third hole and courageously blow a narrow and controlled stream of air. Ah Sweet Lord. It works. **It works!** The band is looking at you with nods of approval.

"Get it on!" shouts the drummer.

You get it on. 4draw to 3blow. 3blow to 4draw.

"Wa Wa Waaaaaaaaaa tat tatta tat!"

You are unbelievably hot. 4 draw. That's your note. Your hot little honey of a note. Play 4draw, play; and **4draw plays.**

You close your eyes and visualize the sounds you hear. All around you the music changes — chords, you suppose — but you play the same two notes and you never make a mistake. You feel as though you were in the eye of a hurri-cane, somehow saved from clashing with the music that roars all around you.

37

You gain confidence. "Maybe it's impossible to make a mistake," you think. You decide to try to play something fancier than just 3blow, 4draw. You play 3blow, 3draw, 4blow, 4draw. You hold 4draw for a long time, warbling and wailing, looking at the band with a triumphant gleam in your eye.

Then you decide to go back down to 3blow. You play 4draw, 4blow — YUCK! WHAT HAPPENED? The 4blow sounded terrible. You slide down over the 3draw to the 3blow — safe at last. Thank God.

The music ends and you modestly lay down your harp. Even though you made that mistake on 4blow, you played pretty darn well. You're jazzed and so is the band. The lead guitar player even says something about your "Primitive feel for the thing, you know what I mean, man. . ." You assure him that you do.

As you leave, the bass player asks if you can make the gig at Annie's Tugboat this Friday night. Playing it coy, you say you'll let him know.

Soon you and the Stallions are playing gigs all over the country and making more money than you know how to spend. One night a talent scout hears you, and within a month, you are signed and recorded. Your album becomes an instant success and "Rolling Stone" heralds you as being the greatest blues player of all time.

Not bad for a beginner. Not bad at all.

PRINCIPLES
OF
CROSS HARP

THE CROSS HARP
DRAW CHORD

A C harmonica means that blowing on holes one, two, three and four at the same time plays a C chord. Drawing on holes one, two, three and four at the same time plays a G chord. In cross harp you play a C harmonica in the key of G. The Cross Harp Draw Chord and its system of Harmonizing and Steppingstone Notes is the musical basis of the blues. Within its structure, the blues harpist creates and resolves tension.

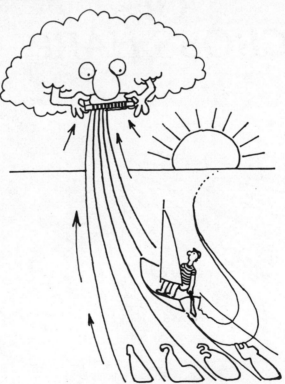

**The Cross Harp Draw Chord
is the root of the blues.**

HARMONIZING NOTES

Chords are made up of Harmonizing Notes. When you play these notes individually they will always fit in with music played in their key. They are Safe Notes — notes which won't make mistakes.

The Cross Harp Harmonizing Notes are 1draw, 2draw, 3draw, 4draw, 6draw and 3blow and 6blow. The notes above 6draw are not practical for beginning harp players.

The Cross Harp Harmonizing Notes are the notes you can depend on. If you are tuned and keyed to a guitarist, taped cassette or record, these notes will always work.

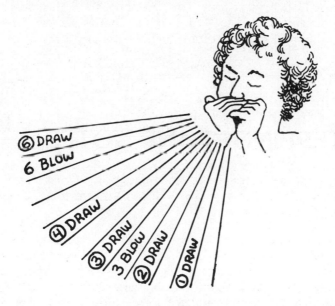

These notes harmonize with
the Cross Harp Draw Chord.

EXPERIMENT WITH HARMONIZING NOTES

Play your Harmonizing Notes as you accompany the guitar music on your taped cassette. If you are tuned and keyed correctly, you will find that any Harmonizing Note will sound good with the music when you play a clear single note. Hold 4draw for a long time, and when your ear tells you to, move to 3blow. Hold 6draw for a long time, and when the time is right (trust your instincts) go to 6blow or 3blow or 1draw.

Play your Harmonizing Notes in any order that you want. After all, this is improvisational harmonica. The main thing at this stage is that you are loosening up and playing these notes with rich, clear tone. Listen to how the notes merge with the guitar. Play softly enough so that as one ear listens to the harmonica, the other one hears the taped cassette.

STEPPINGSTONE NOTES

Steppingstone Notes are not members of the Cross Harp Draw Chord, and this is why you don't accent them. They are important, however.

Playing without Steppingstone Notes is like speaking without the words "and", "if", and "but". Steppingstone Notes serve as connectors between one Safe Note and another. The trick is to glide over them smoothly, with finesse. The Steppingstone Notes are 1blow, 2blow, 3blow, 4blow, 5draw, and 5blow.

If your harmonica playing clashes with the music it is supposed to harmonize with, you either aren't tuned or keyed, or you have just accented a Steppingstone Note.

NOTES OF RESOLUTION AND WAILING NOTES

There are two kinds of Harmonizing Notes: Notes of Resolution and Wailing Notes. Let's look at some pictures to understand what their functions are.

Imagine music as a river. _____

If the guitar is playing in the key of G, then it is a river of G.

G _____

Now suppose we add a harmonica to the river of music.* It begins in the river, rises smoothly from the water, finds a good strong note, holds it for several beats, bending, twisting — WAWAWAWAAH, creating tension.

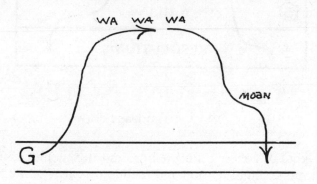

There is a pause, and then the note begins to return to the river. Just when you think it's going to dive back in, it finds another note that is just above the water. The harmonica player holds this note just long enough for a sleepy moan that lasts a couple of beats and creates more tension. Finally, it eases back into the river and releases the tension.

*Remember, in Cross Harp you use a C harp to play in the key of G.

When the harmonica is in the river, it is playing a Note of Resolution. When it is bending and twisting on one note that is out of the river, it is playing a Wailing Note. The notes in between are Steppingstone Notes.

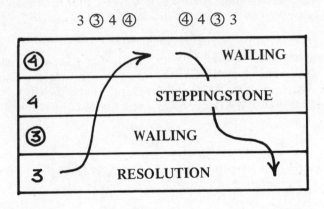

○ means draw

Any kind of cohesive storytelling, and this includes blues, attempts to build tension and then release it. Wailing Notes and Notes of Resolution are both Safe Notes, but Wailing Notes create tension, and Notes of Resolution resolve it. The trick of playing the blues harmonica lies in making tension on your Wailing Notes and resolving the tension on the Notes of Resolution, and moving smoothly from one to the other on Steppingstone Notes.

When you play cross harp on the third and fourth holes, 4draw and 3draw are Wailing Notes. 3blow is the Note of Resolution. 4blow is a Steppingstone Note.

SEEING IS BELIEVING

An essential skill in learning to make music is the ability to visualize sound, i.e., the ability to see music in your inner eye. Visualization requires listening and relaxing. Turn on your stereo and lay yourself down. Once the music starts, close your eyes and open your ears. Focus on the lead instrument. It doesn't matter whether it's a guitar, a harmonica, or a human voice. Visualize the sound that the instrument makes as it goes up and down, as it quivers, as it dies.

A constant tone might look like this:

A constant tone that goes up one step might look like this:

Sometimes a harp or guitar riff happens so quickly that all you can visualize is a confused, scrambled line.

The graphs in this book are visualizations of the fundamental sounds of the blues harmonica. The curved and wiggly lines represent the sound of the harp and the direction that it follows. The framework of the graphs tells you what holes to play in order to get that sound, and whether to blow or draw.

UP AND DOWN BLUES RIFF

This riff uses all the notes in the third and fourth holes.

3 ③ 4 ④ ④ 4 ③ 3

Blow and draw on the third hole. Blow and draw on the fourth hole. 4draw is the Wailing Note, so hold it out and make tension on it. Pause, then draw and blow on the fourth hole, draw on the third hole and resolve the riff on 3blow.

The Up and Down Blues Riff

3 ③ 4 ④ ④ 4 ③ 3

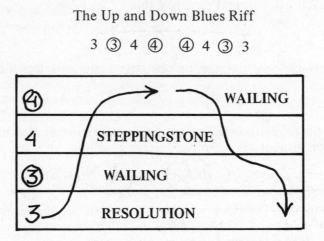

Remember to glide smoothly over 4blow. It is a Stepping-stone Note. When you have created tension on 4draw, your instincts will tell you to blow. Instead of letting all your air out on 4blow, play it smoothly and slide down to 3draw and finally 3blow, where you let out the air and resolve with the same breath.

To make this run sound bluesy you must eliminate the gaps between the notes. This takes a smooth reversal of breath, plus a clean change from three to four and from four to three.

When you can play the Up and Down Blues Riff solo, try it with a record or taped cassette. Stress the 4draw and 3blow. They are the backbone of the pattern and neither note will make a mistake.

Try this in various forms and fashions. Change the accent of the riff by stressing the 4draw one time and the 3draw the next time, by tonguing and by phrasing. Remember to resolve on 3blow so that the changes will make musical sense.

Denying the ear that feeling of resolution is a fun game. It's also the basis of music. When you play with your cassette of taped guitar music, you will notice that there are times when it doesn't sound good to resolve. That's because the guitar is busy denying the ear the resolution at the exact same time that you are resolving.

The trick is to stay on 3draw until your ear tells you to resolve. You have to listen to the music you are accompanying and anticipate chord changes. This anticipation is not an intellectual activity. It is the art of listening.

If you resolve too soon on 3blow, just draw until your ear tells you to try to resolve again. Learning to do this provides a lot of fun for harpist and guitar player. It also leads to some interesting games between 3draw and 3blow.

IMPROVISING

Notice the similarity in the words **improve** and **improvise**. To improvise, you need a theme to improve on. Let the Up and Down Blues Riff be your theme, and let your mistakes be your improvements.

The Up and Down Blues Riff is the basic, unadorned, granddaddy blues and country western harmonica cliché, and before you purposely improve it, you should know it well.

On the other hand, when you make mistakes, just pretend that you know what you are doing, and get to a Safe Note. Mistakes sound great when you don't let them break your confidence and your stride.

ONE WAY TO CONTROL YOUR MISTAKES
IS TO MAKE THEM ON PURPOSE.

Although the Up and Down Blues Riff looks the same on paper everytime you read it, it should not sound the same each time you play it. By changing the accents, timing and feeling of the riff, you bring it to life, and give it meaning.

Harp playing is a lot like singing or whistling. You have to let the music flow through you.

The Up and Down Blues Riff represents the tremendous variety of ways that you can express yourself on 3 ③ 4 ④. . . .④ 4 ③ 3. The next few pages explore the techniques of making music on these notes.

THE UP RIFF

The Up and Down Blues Riff is actually two riffs — The Up Riff and the Down Riff. The Up Riff moves you from the Note of Resolution to the Wailing Note. It is a tension riff.

The Up Riff

3 ③ 4 ④

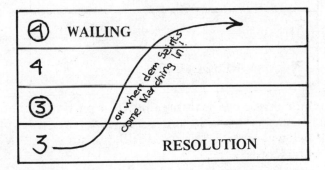

It is also the first line of many a good old song. One of the most famous of these is "Oh When the Saints Come Marching In" as shown above. The Up Riff played three times in a row gets you all the way up to the last line of the song. To follow the melody exactly at this point requires a skilled and dexterous mouth and throat. It's far more realistic for a beginner to continue tonguing to the rhythm of words on 4draw than it is to go searching for the melody.

49

THE DOWN RIFF

The Down Riff brings you down from 4draw. Its most distinguishing characteristic is that it makes the ear expect to hear and the body want to feel the Note of Resolution.

The Down Riff

④ 4 ③ 3

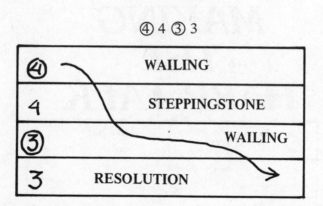

A common mistake in learning this riff is putting too much emphasis on the 4blow. It sometimes works in solo harp, but 4blow will often be the wrong note to stress when you play with records.

Emphasize the Wailing Notes. Make the ear yearn for resolution by sliding over 4blow to 3draw, and accenting the 3draw. It is difficult to understand the tremendous potential of this sequence of notes until you are able to bend 3 draw.

Don't let that dissuade you from practicing this half of the Up and Down Blues Riff. Learn to play a single note every time. Learn to reverse your breath smoothly. Learn to change the phrasing. When you are confident of your single note ability, and the voice of your harmonica is rich and full, you are ready to learn how to bend.

MAKING THE HARP TALK

HANDS

Your hands are magnificent tools for changing the sound that comes out of your harmonica. When they are closed, airtight, they mute the tone, and when they slowly open, your single note says waaa. If you open and close several times, returning to a snug, airtight position each time, your harp says waaa waaa waaa.

Relaxing your fingers makes them more pliable, and this makes the cup more airtight.

Beginners should experiment on 3blow. Remember that it is the movement of the hands that makes the harp sound good, not just being in one position or another. Go smoothly and slowly from closed to open and your note will expand instead of explode.

Fluttering one hand against the other with a gentle clapping motion will produce a warbling effect.

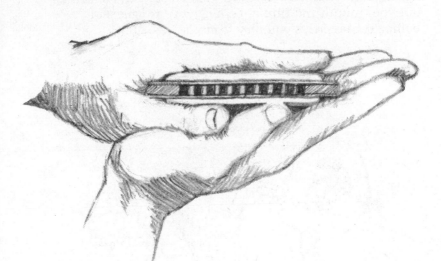

Talk through your harp. Use your hands, tongue, breath, and body to make the harp's voice take on human inflection. Try asking a question through your harp. Plead. Argue. Cry. Bark. Meow. The harp player is an actor. When he plays, he throws out a definite mood or feeling. He speaks his lines in the language of the blues.

BENDING NOTES

Whistling and harp playing are similar in a lot of ways. Like the whistler, the harp player controls his sound by changing the shape of his mouth and throat. The feeling of whistling high and slurring that whistle note down is quite a bit like the feeling of bending notes — except that you can only bend draw notes on your harp. If you start as high as you can whistle and slur down to as low as you can whistle, you will notice how the inhaled stream of air travels from your head down to your voice box. Hollowing out your mouth and throat, arching your tongue and pulling it back helps you play from the voice box.

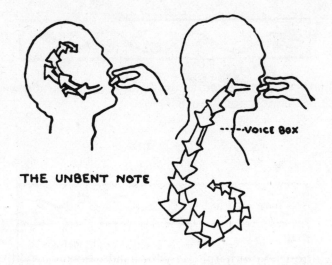

THE UNBENT NOTE

---VOICE BOX

THE BENT NOTE

BENDING 4DRAW

Consider: 4draw, like every other draw note, has a bending potential. This means you can play the note at the top of the bend and you can also bend it down.

The top of the bend is where the ear expects the note to be, so when the harpist bends he is playing games with the senses. It is important that the note is not always played bent down. If it is, it will sound flat. In most cases, when you bend 4draw you should also play the unbent sound of the note.

A tweety bird whistle on the draw will show you how quickly you can bend 4draw.

The top of the Up and Down Blues Riff is a good place to use the Tweety Bird Blues Bend.

The Up Riff

3 ③ 4 ④

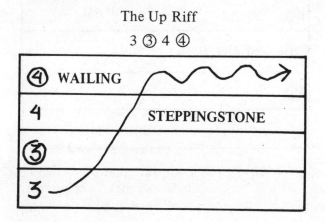

BENDING IN THE UP RIFF

The Start from Bottom Blues Bend is a good way to play
the 4draw in the Up Riff. It helps create the sensation that
4blow and 4draw are connected. This is called **blending**.

Start from Bottom Bend

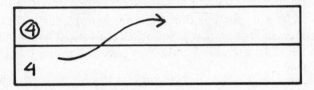

Your hands help create the blending sensation by muffling
the note in the low part of the bend, and fluttering as the
note reaches the top of the bend.

The Up Riff

3 ③ 4 ④

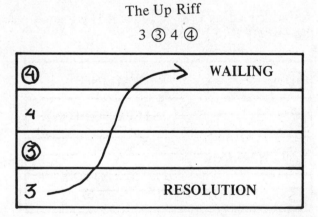

Think of the Up Riff as a question that the Down Riff will
answer. Be sure to pause between riffs. It helps create
tension when you wait for an answer.

BENDING IN THE DOWN RIFF

The Cat's Moan Blues Bend is good for blending 4draw into 4blow. Start low, bring the note up, and curve it down.

Cat's Moan

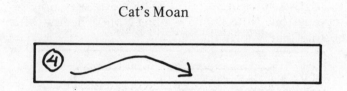

This works well in the second half of the Up and Down Blues Riff. Along with bending skill, blending the 4draw into the 4blow takes a smooth reversal of breath. The riff really sounds great when you catmoan on 3draw and blend it into 3blow.

The Down Riff
④ 4 ③ 3

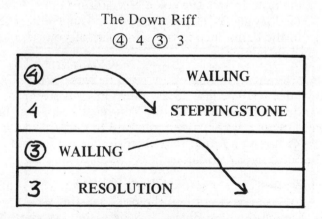

Be sure that you do not peter out on your Note of Resolution. Few things are as frustrating as an unresolute answer to an important question.

THE BEAUTY OF 3DRAW

3draw has a huge bending potential. As a matter of fact, there are two notes in 3draw. The high 3draw is more of a Steppingstone Note than a Wailing Note. The low 3draw is most definitely a Wailing Note.

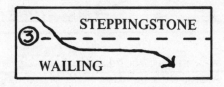

You play the low 3draw by opening your throat and controlling the note from your voice box. I don't mean to use your voice. Playing from the voice box means feeling the note from the harmonica in the same part of your throat that controls talking.

This is different from the 4draw bend because you pull the air down deeper. The low 3draw hums in your stomach much more than the bent 4draw. You must keep your face, lips and tongue relaxed. When you pull the note down into your voice box you'll find that your tongue arches and slips back into your throat.

Your low 3draw might sound a little distorted. This is all right as long as you don't feel the note resisting you as you pull it through the harmonica. The distortion is something you will use purposely as you get better. By inhaling through your nose as well as your mouth you increase your control over your low 3draw.

3DRAW IN THE DOWN RIFF

3draw is a terrific tension note because it blends into 3blow, the Note of Resolution.

The Down Riff

④ 4 ③ 3

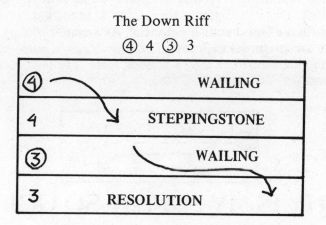

3BLOW AND DRAW JAM

There is a lot of music in the third hole. 3blow is a Note of Resolution and 3draw (low) is a very bluesy Wailing Note. Drive out a rhythm with your tongue on 3blow. When your ear tells you, play a long, low 3draw. You can play it like a moaning locomotive whistle or make it cry like a baby. When you return to 3blow, pick up on your tonguing again. Drive that rhythm home.

3Blow and Draw Jam

3 ③ 3 ③ 3

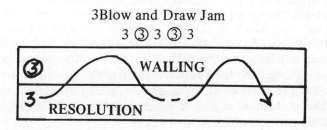

USING 3DRAW AS A STEPPINGSTONE

3draw is normally played as a Steppingstone Note in the
Up Riff. This means play it high, in your head, and
smoothly. Reverse your breath into 4blow and make
your tension on 4draw.

WHY IS MY 3DRAW SO UGLY?

Besides being the bluest note on your harp, 3draw is also
one of the toughest to master. Beginners find that the air
passing through 3draw seems blocked. There is a tendency
to tighten up and suck hard. The result is a vague foghorn
sound, or worse, no sound at all.

The problem is usually rooted in how you form the mouthpiece (your lips) for the single note. It is much harder to
play 3draw, let alone bend it, when your mouth is tight,
your single note hole isn't oval, or your harp isn't well in
your mouth and sealed by the fleshy insides of your lips.

It also helps to open your nasal passages and play 3draw
in your head as well as your body. You really have to be
mellow with 3draw. Coax the air out of the harmonica.
Don't force it. Instead of tightening when you bend, make
a conscious effort to relax. You'll find that the **larger** your
single note hole is, the easier you will play the single notes.
Most beginners make the single note holes too small. They
put their lips on the edge of the harp instead of the tin
plates. That is why their 3draw is ugly.

BODY AND HEAD

This description is stolen from the poor vocal teacher who tried to teach me how to sing. It seems that I couldn't get rid of the bullfrog in my voice. My higher notes were like auto horns and my lower notes compared to the sound of a lowered tractor blade scraping gravel from a cement basketball court.

"Put that note in your body," she'd say to me. Or, "Put that note in your head." I guess it depended on whether she was hearing a traffic jam or a construction site.

I never did learn to vocalize, but I did gain two tidbits of insight into harp playing.

1. It's easier to play the harp than it is to sing.
2. When I play harp, I put some notes in my body and others in my head.

The unbent draw notes strike the roof of my mouth, and I feel a hum in the bones of my head. As I bend the note down I am receptive to the air and even the sound of the note humming in my body. This is a very distinct feeling, as though I have a wa wa pedal in my lungs and an amplifier in my gut.

I don't always play in my body, though. More often, I'm shooting the notes out of my forehead. Nasal passages open, I draw on that note as though my harp were a mint julep inhaler. I can feel the air buzzing in my eyeballs.

QUESTIONS AND ANSWERS

Should I pull the air into my lungs each time I play a draw note?

NO. You should breathe as little as possible. Keep your breath still and satisfied. Make your blows and draws happen with small amounts of air that you control in the front of your mouth.

You have to relax and establish a deep breathing rhythm that can be satisfied as you blow and draw. Talking is all exhale, but a talker rarely gets out of breath because he has balanced his deep breathing needs with the breath control required to form vowels, consonants, words and sentences.

Does it help to tighten up on your low draw notes?

No. You may discover how to bend with the help of tight lips or jaw but tightening up does not actually help you bend. It cramps the tone, creates a hiss, and makes the note cut out on you.

Is tonguing as important as bending?

It's more important. Tonguing creates syllables and phrases out of notes. Tonguing, because of its close association with talking, is an ability that most people have before they ever try to play the harmonica. Every time you say "toot" or "titatat, titatat" you are tonguing your voice. Notice that the flick of your tongue seems to space your voice and give it rhythm. Titatating your breath on 3blow will show you how effectively your tongue punctuates.

ONE NOTE BOOGIE

You can accompany an entire song
playing no other note than 4draw.

You can make 4draw talk by bending it, shaping it with
your hands, and tonguing. There's no need to always make
it a part of a riff. Remember that your goal is to stress the
Harmonizing Notes. You can stress 4draw simply by holding
it for several beats, or by inventing a little phrase that you
repeat consistently throughout the music. Try to imitate
human speech on 4draw. When your ear tells you to change,
play the Down Riff to your Note of Resolution.

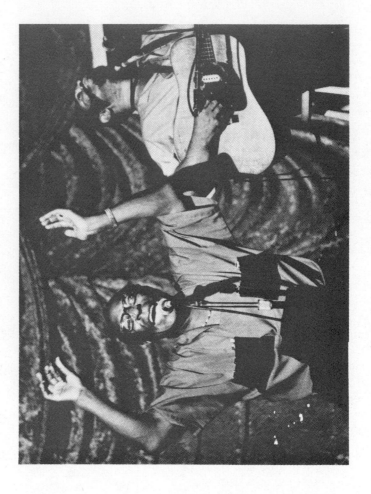

Photo of Sonny and Brownie taken by Lynn Rybarczyk.

ADVANCED
CROSS HARP

THE CROSS HARP MAP COLORING BOOK

Wailing Notes should be colored blue
Notes of Resolution orange
Steppingstone Notes green

⑥	WAILING
6	RESOLUTION
⑤	STEPPINGSTONE
5	STEPPINGSTONE
④	WAILING
4	STEPPINGSTONE
③	WAILING
3	RESOLUTION
②	RESOLUTION
2	STEPPINGSTONE
①	WAILING
1	STEPPINGSTONE

THE UPPER NOTES

Suppose you want to break away from the single note patterns we've worked on so far. What do you do? Take a riff you already know.

The Up Riff

3 ③ 4 ④

Add a little life to it by sliding the harmonica over Stepping-stone Note 5draw to Wailing Note 6draw. The draw slide has the effect of someone running his hand up the keys of a piano. All you have to do is continue drawing as you slide the harp to 6draw.

The Upper Riff

3 ③ 4 ④ ➔ ⑥ 6

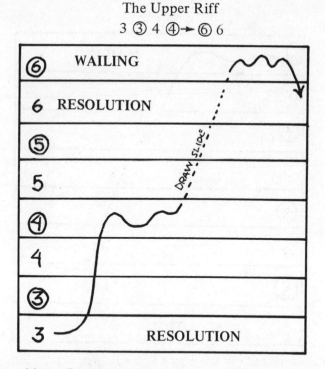

Wail on 6draw. Punctuate by bending or tonguing. Resolve the tension on 6blow.

6blow and 6draw have the same relationship as 3blow and 3draw — except that you don't have to bend 6draw down to create tension. This means that you can solo or accompany entirely on the sixth hole, creating tension on the 6draw and resolving the tension on 6blow.

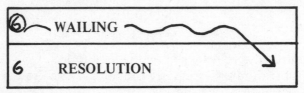

After wailing on 6draw, you can resolve on 3blow via the Blues Scale Down.

Blues Scale Down
⑥ 6 ⑤ ④ 4 ③ 3

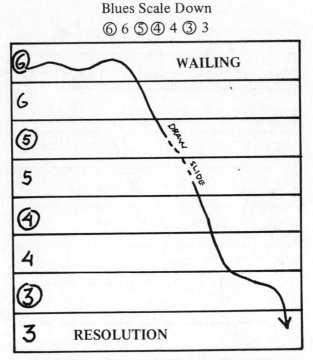

Treat every note in the Blues Scale Down, except 3draw, as a chain of Steppingstone Notes. At 3draw, bend your sound down to 3blow for a smooth ending to a great aerial ride.

6blow is a Note of Resolution. It's up an octave from 3blow and 2draw. The Surprise Resolution on the Down Riff will make this clearer.

Surprise Resolution
④ 4 ③ 6

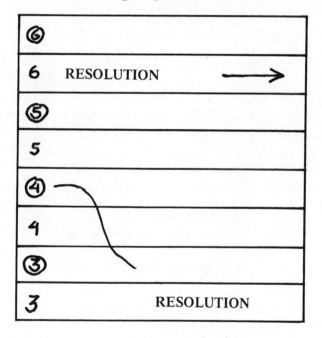

THE LOW NOTES

The Harmonizing Notes on holes one and two are 1draw and 2draw. 2draw is the Note of Resolution. It is the same note as 3 blow. The advantage of 2draw is that you can bend it. It has a huge bending potential. High 2draw is the Note of Resolution. Low 2draw is a very bluesy Steppingstone.

```
┌─────────────────────────────────┐
│        RESOLUTION               │
│  ②-─ ── ── ── ── ──┐            │
│                                 │
│      STEPPINGSTONE              │
└─────────────────────────────────┘
```

A popular blues harp technique is to create tension by bending 2draw down into low 2draw and slowly bringing it back up.

Barrel-Scraper Bend

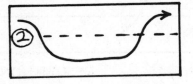

2draw is as difficult to bend as 3draw. If you tighten up or suck hard, the sound of the note will cut out on you. Before attempting the bend 2draw, you should be sure that you can play it unbent.

70

THE GOOD MORNING RIFF

The Good Morning Riff can be played slow or fast. It is the basic cross harp move for the bottom end of your harp.

The Good Morning Riff

① 2 ②

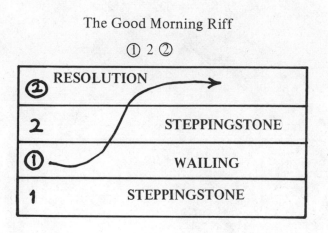

② RESOLUTION	
2	**STEPPINGSTONE**
①	**WAILING**
1	**STEPPINGSTONE**

The Good Morning Riff sounds best when the 1draw isn't bent. Play all the notes in your head and use the Barrel Scraper Bend on 2draw when you want to add extra tension.

Because 1draw, 2draw, 3draw, and 4draw are all Safe Notes, you can move around pretty freely. Even if you play two notes at the same time by mistake, it will sound good if you keep the accent on the draw.

The Good Morning Riff is a good pattern to repeat over and over to the same rhythm, altering the feeling a little bit each time. A good way to do this is to tongue 2draw to a basic rhythm, and work the Good Morning Riff in.

WILLIE'S BEST FRIEND

Ol' Willie tottered down the tracks. He'd been on the road for thirteen days, hitchin' and ridin' from D.C. all the way to Abilene. Now he was hoping that a train would come by so he could get the hell out of Texas too. He sat down on the gravel where the tracks ran and crossed his legs. He listened to the north and he listened to the south, but he didn't hear the clickity clack of the ol' locomotive or woooo! wooooooo! whistle that sometimes blew so lightly in the distance before a train came.

"Well, hell," Ol' Willie said. "Guess I'll have to play me some blues."

The sun had been burning down since morning and the sweat poured down Ol' Willie's face as he took his harp out of the bottom of his knapsack.

"Sure am lonely, ol' harp," said Willie. "Sure am lonely." And he began to play.

"Wawaaaaaaaaaaaaaa. Titditti wa wa."

"Oh yeah, them ol' sick heart blues!" sang Willie. "Oh yeah! Miss my baby!"

"Wa waaaaah wa titti ti was tidot dot tood oddy!" sang the harp.

Ol' Willie played the sad blues for a long time. Then it seemed that he'd played all the sadness right out of himself. There wasn't any more. "Well, hell," Ol' Willie said. "Guess I'll have to play me a little Freight Harp."

He started dancing right there on the tracks, hopping from tie to tie, shuffling over the long rail.

"See that train going down the track.
Took my baby, she ain't coming back."

Then he started playing a railroad train out of his harmonica. He played the tracks and he played the wheels and he played the big pistons charging up and down and he played the whistle woooo woooooo wooooooh!

He played for a long time. The sun got hotter. The sweat poured down his face. He started getting lonely for a drink of water.

"Mr. Harmonica," Willie finally said to the harp, "Sometimes I think you're the only one who cares what happens to ol' Willie." He thumped the harp gently on the palm of his hand. "And here I don't even have no box to put you in."

He looked sadly across the hot Texas countryside and listened for the faint cry of a whistle. It didn't come.

Willie picked up his knapsack and looked far down the tracks. The sun was bright, and he wiped the sweat from his shining face. "Sure hope the train comes soon," he said as he gently put the harmonica back in the knapsack and began his long walk down the railroad tracks.

GETTING IT ON WITH
HARMONICA CHORDS

Some of the best harp music is train-time music played in a
fast rhythmic shuffle on the chords on your harmonica.
The trick is to start with a slow draw blow draw blow
breathing pattern on the bottom four holes of your harp,
tonguing a trainlike rhythm on the Cross Harp Draw
Chord. Once you've established a pattern and a feeling,
begin picking up your tempo, like a train picking up speed.

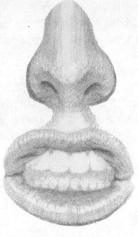

To make your chords sound like church organs instead of
traffic jams your mouth must be large and relaxed. The harp
should be touching your teeth and air must escape through
the space between your upper lip and the top of the harp.
In other words, loosen up. Forget the airtight seal. In chords
you let the air leak. Now just breathe in and out, draw and
blow, draw and blow. Be sure to breathe shallowly so you
don't faint from hyperventilation.

Treat the Cross Harp Draw Chord as a Note of Resolution. Make it louder than the Blow Chord and play it for a long time. Accent it.

The Blow Chord is a Steppingstone Chord. Be sure that you don't play it loud and hard. If you are having trouble getting rid of air remember to blow it over the top of the harp as well as into the harp.

Once you've gotten so you can control your breathing you should try to fit your draw chord in with the guitar on your taped cassette. You'll find that tonguing helps fit the draw chord into the rhythm, and keeping the blow chord soft and short keeps the harmonica from clashing with the guitar. Practicing very softly, with small amounts of air, also makes it easier. Try to eliminate gaps between the draw and blow, the blow and draw. The tonguing on the draw note should be crisp, but the syllables shouldn't be choppy.

PLAYING THE HARP WITHOUT THE HARP

Why not? Get some music started with your feet and your breath. Snap your fingers. Turn yourself into a human percussion instrument.

Your mouth, tongue and breath are capable of a lot of sounds. It's remarkable how coordinated we are in there.

Have you ever heard John Mayall's "Room to Move" with his **chicka chicka chicka chicka**? He is playing harp without the harp.

TRAIN-TIME TONGUING PATTERN

Say the sounds "ah taaah ta." Now whistle these sounds on the inhale. Notice that you get three syllables. This is a popular tonguing pattern for fast, rhythmic train music.

WALKIN' THE HARP

An easy way to turn onto some good rhythms is to take your harp for a walk. Your body is a natural rhythm machine and your feet slap the pavement in musical time. Count it out -1-2-3-4 — 1-2-3-4-. After you've counted a few minutes, the machine should be chugging along under its own steam. Even if you stopped walking the machine would keep going if you wanted it to.

Get a breathing and tonguing pattern going that fits your walking rhythm.

Breathing rhythm:	(1234)	1234	(1234)	1234
Walking rhythm:	1	2	3	4
Tonguing Pattern:	ahtaata		ahtaata	

Remember to accent the Cross Harp Draw Chord.

Breathe air over the top of your harp.

Breathe superficially.

Eliminate gaps between draws and blows.

Keep your nasal passages open.

Breathe from your head.

Pretend you're a locomotive.

78

APPLICATION

AN UNDERSTANDING

The Up and Down Blues Riff, the Cross Harp Draw Chord, the Good Morning Riff, and the runs that take you up to 6draw and down again are the basic moves of simple country and blues harmonica. Reading the runs on a piece of paper, or out of a book, and playing them on your harp will not automatically produce music. You should practice until you no longer think of them in terms of numbers and concepts. Practicing helps you internalize the runs so that they come out in their own natural, unselfconscious way. When this happens, you will be playing by sound and feeling instead of rote and memorization. The result will be music.

Many of the riffs that the best harp players use are far more complex than anything that has been discussed in these pages. They are so complex, in fact, that writing them down is a complete waste of time. You will discover your own complexities by working on the riffs in this book, making mistakes, and saying to yourself, "Hey! That sounds pretty good. How did I do that?"

Complex runs, incidentally, do not necessarily sound better than simple runs. The most important single factor in harp playing is the tone of the harmonica. If you have a clear, throbbing voice, nobody cares whether your runs are complex or simple.

It is difficult to take a memorized run and stick it into music. Often it isn't appropriate, or the fact that it is memorized makes you so self-conscious that you can't play it well. When you start out playing with the records listed in this book, you should start simply, remembering the importance of 3blow and 4draw. Once you can make these notes work, you can begin filling in the details by using the Up Riff and the Down Riff and as many variations as you can discover.

80

The success of your harmonica playing depends, to a great extent, on your ability to follow through on your mistakes. If you do accent a Steppingstone Note and it clashes with the music, you should keep right on going.

There are exceptions to almost every explanation in these pages. Steppingstone Notes sometimes sound good. Bob Dylan doesn't always play with single notes, his tone is often poor, and he's a great harp player. Some harp players play their country and blues music on straight harp. Although the holes above 6draw are generally impractical for beginners, some harpists make good use of them.

The principles of harmonica playing that are described in this book do not pretend to be the end-all-be-all definition of good music. They simply provide a system, a way of thinking about harmonica playing that works. Understand that the goal of the system is to help you learn to make music and have fun on the harmonica as soon and as often as possible.

A HARP PLAYER'S DREAM - PART II

You hear them shout your name and you walk out on the stage with nothing but your G harp. The applause is deafening. Rose petals fly through the air. You raise your arms and suddenly the Coliseum is as quiet as a church. You put the harp to your mouth and play a low moan of a 4draw. The audience leans forward. They recognize your beat, your tone, your feel. They love you.

Together you pound out the rhythm. They with their clapping hands, and you with the stomping of your boot heel on an old fruit box. Nothing fancy, just 1-2-3-4-1-2-3-4 -1-2-3-4.

You are still on 4draw, your hands warbling the note as it sails upward towards the top of its bend. You pause. It's a dramatic moment as the beat plods forward and you hesitate. Suddenly. . .waaaaaa! It's a 6draw, a complete surprise to everyone, even yourself, and it's playing clear and strong, bending tweety bird style, raising the tension to new heights. Wah wah wah! it cries. Wah wah wah!

82

Suddenly you shoot down over 6blow and 5draw to 4draw to 4blow to. . .My God! people in the audience suddenly realize, it's the Blues Scale Down. . .to 3draw, which you bend down cat's moan style to 3blow.

The audience is up on its feet. You know you've got them going, so you double up on the rhythm of their clapping hands, fitting notes between their beats, and tonguing a train pattern on your Cross Harp Draw Chord, moving around the harp at will — 6draw here, 3draw there. Then you go into the Good Morning Riff alternating it with wild draw slides on your harmonica clear up to 6draw. The beat continues. Your harmonica moans, growls, cries and laughs and plays like a train racing across the countryside.

Silence in the Coliseum. Silence as you walk down from the stage. Silence as you disappear into your dressing room. Starting with a ripple, and slowly building, the applause grows like a giant wave of human souls who love you for the joy and happiness that you have brought into the world.

Dream on, ol' harp buddy. Dream on.

83

PLAYING WITH RECORDS

Once you can play a single note consistently on the Beginner's Blues Riff, you should begin accompanying records. Find a song on one of the following albums that you like, and select the right key harp for it. Play the song over and over. Imagine a harp accompaniment. Then, playing your harp, explore the principles described in these pages.

Start out by playing along in 4draw, and make sure that it harmonizes. If it sounds pretty good, slide down to 3blow.

Toot along on these notes until you feel confident enough to try the Up and Down Blues Riff. Remember the importance of a clear single note. Once it starts to fade, stop, and rest your lip. Give it a massage. Relax.

PLAYING WITH FOLKS

Playing with folks is more difficult than playing with records. This is mainly because of the human factor. A record is a predictable medium. You can stop it, and start it. You can control its volume. You can turn it off.

People aren't so easily controlled. Guitarists sometimes change key, or they don't tune up to you, or they give you a dirty look each time you start to play. Playing with folks can be frustrating and hard. It's also one of the most rewarding, fun ways to spend an evening that I know. Harp and guitar are made for each other. No other two instruments jam quite as effectively.

Here are some clues to help your jam come off.

84

Take responsibility for yourself. Know what key the music is in so you can play the appropriate harp. Be certain that the guitar is in tune with the harp. Few things sound as rancid as two out of tune instruments trying to play with each other.

Start simply. The easiest way to enter a song is to play a long Wailing Note. 4draw is probably the best for a beginner. Just fit the note in, and listen for the music telling you to resolve.

Communicate with your guitarist. Watch his hands and his face. Try to get a feeling for HIS music, his rhythm, his style.

Fake it. If you are tuned and keyed, and remember to play with the accent on the draw, you cannot make a mistake. With the exception of 5draw, all draw notes on holes one through six are safe.

Repeat simple patterns. Remember that music is made up of patterns and variations of these patterns. Find a simple theme that works with the guitar and repeat it, changing the timing and feeling when appropriate.

Don't play continuously. Phrase your riffs. Use silence to build expectations. Understand that some songs might sound better with very little harp in them. Sometimes it's more appropriate to sing along, or play rhythm on the back of an empty guitar case. A good harp player will sometimes let a song start without him, and play only in the last part. This helps the song build instead of being one constant, unchanging parade of sound.

Don't hog the lead. But when you take it, take it! Unless the musicians, yourself included, are pretty hot, only one instrument should take the lead at a time. Lead guitar players are notorious for hogging the lead. Sometimes the best way to deal with them is to ask them to shut up for a few bars so you can get some of your licks in.

Try to make the other musicians sound good. Understand that the harp has its limitations. Don't be a star. Play harmonica so that it enhances the efforts of others.

Don't expect too much. Even the best musicians have to be patient with one another. It always takes a few sessions to get your act together.

A WORD ON STRAIGHT HARP

A good harmonica player plays straight harp as well as cross harp. The reason this book hasn't said much about straight harp is that most folks figure it out for themselves. As soon as they start trying to figure out a melody, they find they are playing straight harp, i.e., playing music in the key that it says on their harmonica and accenting the blow notes instead of the draw.

**Blowing on holes 1234 at the same time
plays the Straight Harp Blow Chord.**

The Straight Harp Blow Chord is the basis of straight harp
harmonica music. You play this chord by blowing on holes
one, two, three and four at the same time. If you have a
C harp, this will produce a C chord. On a D harp, it will
produce a D chord. All the blow notes on your harmonica
harmonize with the Straight Harp Blow Chord. The Notes
of Resolution in straight harp are 1blow, 4blow, 7blow,
and 10blow.

The disadvantage of playing a harmonica style that stresses
the blow notes is that blow notes (especially the lower
ones) cannot be bent. Bending is an important technique in
creating tension and playing riffs that have a bluesy feel. It
is not so important in playing melodies, and making mellow
accompaniment. There are times, in fact, when bending is
downright inappropriate. These are the times to play
straight harp.

The keys of harmonica that are listed for each song in the Record Index are for playing cross harp. If you want to play straight harp with any of the songs on these records, you will have to perform a minor computation. If you read the section on tuning and keying, you will remember that the harp player selects the correct harmonica for playing cross harp by asking what key the guitar is playing in and counting up four keys, including that particular key.

Guitar Key			Cross Harp Key
A	B	C	D
1	2	3	4

To play cross harp in the key of A, you'd play a D harmonica. To play straight harp in the key of A, you'd play an A harmonica. Since the harp listings in the Record Index are for playing cross harp, if you want to play straight harp, you'll have to count backwards four keys from the key that is listed.

For example, the Record Index says that you need a C harmonica to play cross harp with Tom T. Hall's song, "Me and Jesus Got Our Own Thing Going." If you want to play straight harp with that song, you should count backwards four keys from the key of C.

C B A G
4 3 2 1

And play a G harp with the accent on the blow.

You can avoid making this computation (though it isn't very difficult) by consulting the chart in "Tuning and Keying."

MELODIES

Simple melodies make good harp music, particularly when you're sitting around the campfire or kitchen with friends. Most of the old-timers that follow are played straight harp. For these songs, guitar or piano accompaniment should be in the key it says on your harmonica.

Tonguing (see "Boogie," page 21) is an important skill in melody playing. If the word is "sunshine" on 5blow, simply play a 5blow and make a tata tonguing motion against the roof of your mouth. This makes the harp say "sunshine." If the word is "Shenandoah" on 4blow, say ta ta tata. If you have a good single note, your harp will sing "Shenandoah" as clear and rich as any voice.

Because there are notes missing on your harmonica between 2blow and 2draw, and between 3blow and 3draw, some of these melodies require that you bend 2draw or 3draw down to hit that missing note. This is notated by a circle with an arrow. Bending to play the missing note instead of just bending to create an effect is an advanced harmonica technique. The trick is to get that note bent so it's right on key and doesn't sound distorted.

You can often avoid the problem of not having the right notes on your harmonica by playing the song on the high end of your harp, i.e., holes 6 through 10. The order of your notes reverses above 6draw. (See "Your Harp," page 17.) This means that blow notes are higher than draw notes. You'll find that you can bend the blow notes, especially 8blow, by wiggling your airstream as you push it into your harmonica.

This is similar to the Tweety Bird Blues Bend on the blow.

89

Beginners will discover that they can play some of these melodies without getting a single note. Bob Dylan, for instance, often plays melodies without single notes. He simply makes his mouthpiece large enough to get two or three notes at the same time. The song is then played in chords (groups of harmonizing note) instead of only single notes. You can mix the two techniques as you go along, playing part of the song in chords and other part in single notes.

You can also tongueblock when you play these melodies. Make your mouth large enough to get two, three, or four notes at the same time. Then cover every hole with the tip of your tongue, except the hole you want to play. By lifting your tongue you play a chord that harmonizes with your single note. And by covering the holes with your tongue, you play your single note. Tongueblocking can turn your harmonica into a pipe organ.

◯ **Means draw.**

◯ **Means draw and bend down.**

90

Oh Susannah   *Straight Harp*

4 ④ 5   6   ⑥6 5   4   ④   5   ④ 4   ④
Well I come from Alabama with my banjo on my knee

4 ④   5 6   ⑥6 5 4 ④ 5   4   ④   4
An' I'm going to Louisiana oh my true love for to see.

⑤   ⑥   ⑥   6   5 4 ④
Oh Susannah! Oh don't you cry for me.

4 ④   5   6   ⑥6 5 4 ④ 5 4   ④   4
For I'm bound for Louisiana oh my true love for to see.

You Are My Sunshine   *Straight Harp*

3   4 ④ 5   5 ④ 5   4
You are my sunshine, my only sunshine

4   ④   5 ⑤ ⑥ ⑥   6 ⑤ 5
You make me happy when skies are grey

4   ④ 5 ⑤   ⑥ ⑥   6 ⑤ 5 4
You'll never know dear how much I love you

4   ④   5   ⑤   ④   5 4
Please don't take my sunshine away

Swing Low, Sweet Chariot   *Cross Harp*

③   3   ③   3 2 ①   3   ③④ 5   ④
Swing low, sweet chariot coming for to carry me home.

5 ④③   ④   3 2 ①   3   ③ 3   2   3
Swing low, sweet chariot coming for to carry me home.

91

Polly Wolly Doodle   *Straight Harp*

4 ④ 5   4   ④ 5   4
Oh I went down South for to see my gal

4 ④ 5   ⑤   5 ④
Singing polly wolly doodle all day

③ ④ ③ ④   ③
My Sal she is a spunky gal

③   6   ⑤   ④ 4
Singing polly wolly doodle all day

4   ④ 5 4 ④ 5
Fare thee well, fare thee well

4   ④ 5   ⑤ 5 ④
Fare thee well my fairy fay   .

③ 4 ④   ③   4 ④   ③
For I'm bound to Louisiana for to see my Susianna

③   6   ⑤   ④ 4
Singing polly wolly doodle all day

Clementine   *Straight Harp*

4   3   5   4   4   5   6   ⑤   5   ④
Oh my darlin', oh my darlin', oh my darlin', Clementine.

④   5   ⑤·   5   ④5   4   4   5   ④3 ③   ④   4
You are lost and gone forever. Dreadful sorry Clementine.

Ol' Stewball   *Straight Harp*

3   4   ④   5   ④   4   3   4   ④   5   ④
Ol' Stewball was a racehorse. An' I wish he were mine.

④   5   ⑤   5④ ③   4   ④   4
He never drank water. He only drank wine.

Shenandoah   *Straight Harp*

3   4   ④ 5   ⑤ ⑥   6   7⑦⑥   6   ⑥ 6 5 6
Oh Shenandoah, I love to wander. Away, you rolling river.

5 6 ⑥   5 6   5④   4   4   ④5   4   5   ⑥ 6
Oh Shenandoah, I love to wander. Look away. Oh look away.

   4   ④   5   4④ 4
Cross the wide Missouri.

Hallelujah I'm A Bum   *Straight Harp*

6 ⑥ 6   5 ④ 4
Hallelujah, I'm a bum

6 ⑥ 6   5 6 ④
Hallelujah, bum again!

6 ⑥ 6   5 ④   4
Hallelujah, give us a handout

④   5 ⑤ 5 ④˙ 4
And revive us again

Freight Train   *Straight Harp*

6   5   ④   4 ③ ⑥ 6
Freight train, freight train goin' so fast

6   ⑤   5   ④ 4 6 5
Freight train, freight train goin' so fast

5 ⑤ 5 ④   4 ④ 4
Please don't say what train I'm on

4 ④ 5   4   ④ 5④ 4
And they won't know where I've gone.

Words and music to "Freight Train" used with permission of the composer, Elizabeth Cotten.

94

Wabash Cannonball   *Straight Harp*

6   7   8
I stood on the Atlantic Ocean

8   ⑧ 7 ⑥
On the wide Pacific Shore

6   ⑦   ⑧
Heard the Queen of mountains

⑦   ⑥   6
To the South Bay by the door

6   7   8
She's long, she's tall and handsome

8   ⑧ 7 ⑥
She's loved by one and all

6   ⑦ ⑧
She's the modern combination

⑦   6 ⑥ ⑦ 8
Called the Wabash Cannonball

Hard, Ain't It Hard   *Straight Harp*

5   ④   4   ④ 5 ⑤
It's hard and it's hard, ain't it hard

6   ⑥   6 5 ④
To love someone who never did love you

5   ④ 4   ④ 5 ⑤   ⑥
Hard and it's hard, and it's hard, great God!

5   4   ④   5 ④ 4
To love someone who never will be true

Wildwood Flower   *Straight Harp*

5 ⑤   6   ⑥   7 5   ⑤   5 ④   5   ④   4
I will twine and will mingle my waving black hair

5   ⑤ 6 ⑥ 7 5   ⑤   5 ④ 5 ④ 4
With the roses so red and the lily so fair

6 7 8   ⑧   7   6 ⑥ 7   ⑥   6
The myrtle so green of a bright emerald hue

4 ④ 5 6 ⑥ 6 5 4   ④   5   ④ 4
The pale emanita, and eyes look so blue

Camptown Races   *Straight Harp*

6   5 6 ⑥ 6 5 5 ④ 5 ④
Camptown ladies sing this song doo dah doo dah.

6   5   6 ⑥ 6   5 ④ 5 ④ 4
Camptown racetrack five miles long. Oh doo dah day.

4   5 6 7   ⑥   7 ⑥ 6
Gonna run all night. Gonna run all day.

6   5   6 ⑥ 6 5 ④   5 ⑤ 5 ④ 4
Bet my money on a bob-tail nag. Somebody bet on the bay.

Amazing Grace   *Straight Harp*

3 4 5 5   ④ 4   3
Amazing grace, how sweet the sound

3   4 5 5   ④ 6
That saved a wretch like me

6 ⑥ 6 5 ④ 4   3
I once was lost but now am found

3   4 5   ④ 4
Was blind but now I see.

Old Folks at Home   *Straight Harp*

5   ④ 4 5 ④ 4   7 ⑥ 7
Way down upon the Swannee River

6   5 4 ④
Far, far away

5   ④   4 5 ④ 4   7 ⑥ 7
That's where my heart is turning over

6   5 4 ④   4
That's where the old folks stay

Frankie and Johnny   *Straight Harp*

  4 ④ 5 ⑥ 6 ⑥   4
Frankie and Johnny were lovers

4 ④ 5 ⑥ 6 ⑥   4
Oh Lordy how they could love

7   ⑥ 6 7   ⑥ 6
They swore to be true to each other

7   ⑦ ⑥ 6
True as the stars above

5 6 ⑥ ④ 6   ⑥ 6 5   4
He was her man, but he was doing her wrong

My Horses Ain't Hungry   *Straight Harp*

5   4   ③ 3   ③ 4   5
My horses ain't hungry, they won't eat your hay

5   4   ③ 3   ③ 4 ④ 4
So fair you well Polly, I'm going away

8   7   ⑥ 6   6 ⑥ 7   8
Your parents don't like me, they say I'm too poor

8   7   ⑥ 6   ⑥ 7 ⑧ 7
They say I'm not worthy to enter your door

Cripple Creek   *Straight Harp*

7   6   ⑥   6
I gotta gal at the head of the creek

5   4   5   ④   4
Going up to see her about 8 times a week

7   6   ⑥   6
Kiss her on the mouth just as sweet as any wine

5   4   5   ④   4
Wrap her arms around me like a sweet tater vine

5   ④   4   5   6
Goin' up to Cripple Creek, going in a run

5   ④   4   5   ④   4
Goin' up to Cripple Creek to have some fun

5   ④   4   5   6
Going up to Cripple Creek, going in a whirl

5   ④   4   5   ④   4
Going up to Cripple Creek to see my girl

Roving Gambler   *Straight Harp*

4   5   6   6 ⑥ 6   5 4 5
I am a roving gambler, I've gambled all around

 5   ④ 4   ④   4   5
Wherever I meet with a deck of cards I lay my money down

④   5   ④ 4
I lay my money down

Red River Valley   *Straight Harp*

 3   4   5   ④   5 ④ 4
From this valley they say you are going

 3   4   5   4   5   6   ⑤   5   ④
We will miss your bright eyes and sweet smile

6   ⑤ 5   ④ 4 ④ 5 6   ⑤
For they say you are taking the sunshine

 3   3   ③ 4 ④ 5 ④ 4
That has brightened our pathways awhile

Banks of the Ohio   *Straight Harp*

4   5   4   5   ④
I asked my love to take a walk

④   5   ⑤   6   ⑥ 6   5
Just a little walk, just a little walk

 5   6   ⑥   6   ⑤
Down beside where the waters flow

 4   ④   5   3   5   ④   4
Down by the banks of the Ohio

On Top of Old Smoky *Straight Harp*

4   5   6   7   ⑥
On top of Old Smoky

6   ⑤   6   ⑥   6
All covered with snow

4   5   6   ④
I lost my true lover

5   ⑤   5   4   4
A-courtin' too slow.

Bill Bailey   *Straight Harp*

  5   (4) 5   (4) 5 6
Won't you come home Bill Baily

  5   5   (4) 4
Won't you come home?

  6   5   6 (6) (4)
She cried the whole night long

(5)   5 (5) 5 (5) 6 (5)   5 (5)
I'll do the dishes, honey, I'll pay the rent

6   (6) 6   5
I know I've done you wrong

5   (4) 5 (4) 5 6 5   (4) 5
'Member that rainy evening I drove you out

7   (8) 7 (6)
With nothing but a fine tooth comb

7   (6) 7   8   (6)
Well I know I'm to blame. Well ain't that a shame

7   (6) 7 (6) 8   7
Bill Bailey won't you please come home?

When The Saints Go Marching In   *Straight Harp*

4   5   ⑤   6   4 5   ⑤ 6
Oh when those Saints go marchin' in

4   5   ⑤   6   5 4   5 ④
Oh when those Saints to marching in

5   ④ 4   5 6   ⑤
Lord I want to be in that number

5   ⑤ 6   5 4   ④ 4
When the Saints go marching in

When The Saints Go Marchin' In — *Cross Harp*

3   ③   4   ④ 3 ③   4 ④
Oh when those Saints go marching in

3   ③   4   ④ ③ 3   ③ ③↘
Oh when those Saints go marchin' in

③   ③↘ 3   ③ ④   4
Oh Lord I want to be in that number

③   4   ④ ③ 3   ③↘ 3
When the Saints go marchin' in

○ means draw

104

Summertime — *Straight Harp*

8   7 8 ⑧ 7 ⑧ 8 7 ⑥ 5
Summertime and the living is easy

8   7 ⑧   7   ⑧ 7 ⑦
The fish are jumping, and the cotton is high

8   7 8 ⑧ 7 ⑧ 8 7 ⑥ 5
Your Daddy's rich, and your Ma is good-looking

5 6 5 6 ⑥ 7 8 ⑧ 7 ⑥
So hush little darling don't you cry

Summertime — *Cross Harp*

④ ③﹨④ 1 ③﹨4 ④③② ①
Summertime, and the livin' is easy

④ ③﹨ 4 ③﹨   ④
Fish are jumping and the cotton is high

④ 4 ③﹨④ 4 ③ 4 ④ ③ ② ①
Your Daddy's rich, and your Ma is good looking

① ②﹨①②② ③﹨4 ④ 4 ③﹨ ②
So hush little darling, don't you cry

Q﹨ means draw and bend down

Cocaine Blues   *Straight Harp*

6   4 ④ 5 5 ④ 4
Coke's for horses, not for men

3 ③ 4 ④ 5 ④ 4
They say it's going to kill me

5   ④ 4
But they don't say when

④ 5 ④ 4 5 ④ 4
Cocaine — running round my brain

Sixteen Tons — *Cross Harp*

① 2 ① ② ② ③ ① 2 ② ② ② ①
I loaded sixteen tons and what did I get?

3 ③   ② ① 2 ②   ①
Another day older and deeper in debt

① 2 ②   ③ ② ③ 4
Saint Peter don't you call me, 'cause I can't go

④ 6 ⑤ ④ 4 ③ ②   ②
I owe my soul to the company store.

Stealin' — *Cross Harp*

③   3   ③ 3 ③   3 ③ 3③   3
Put your arms around me like a circle round a sun

①   2   ②③ 3 ③ 3   3   3 ③   3
You know I'm gonna love you when the easy ridings done

③   3 ③④ ③ ② ②   ②
You don't believe I love you, look what a fool I've been

③   3 ③④③ ② ②   ②
You don't believe I love her, look at the hole I'm in

③
Stealin'

④
Stealin'

④   4 3 ③   3
Pretty Mama doncha' tell on me

3 ③   ④   4 ③ 3
I'm stealing back to my same old used to be's

Additional riff

(④ 4 ③ 4 ③ 3 3 ① ①)

Lonesome Valley *Straight Harp*

5   ④ 4   ③ 3
You've got to walk that lonesome valley

5   4 ④ 3 5 ④ 4
You've got to walk it by yourself

5 ④ 4 ③ 4   ④ 4 5 4
Nobody else can walk it for you

3   ③ 3 ⑤ ④ 6 5 ④ 4
You've got to walk it all by yourself

8   7   ⑥ 6
My mama walked that lonesome valley

8   ⑧ 7 8 ⑧ 7
She had to walk it by herself

8 ⑧ 7 ⑥ 7   ⑧ 7 8 7
Nobody else could walk it for her

6 ⑥ 6 ⑨ ⑧ 9 8 ⑧ 7
She had to walk it all by herself

CROSS HARP BLUES CYCLE

The following runs can be played individually, repeated over and over to create a theme, or played in the order presented to create a blues cycle or song.

Standard Blues Riff

④ 4 ③ 4 ③ 3 3

Tuba Blues Riff

2 3 2 1

Fancy Standard Blues Riff

3 ③ 4 ④ 4 ③ 4 ③ 3 3

(Note: The Fancy Standard Blues Riff is the same as the Standard Blues Riff, except that it has an introduction of

3 ③ 4 . . .)

Berkeley Blues Riff

3 ③ 4 <u>④ ④ ④ ⑤ ④</u> 4 ④

(Note: The underlined notes are all on the draw. You can either tongue or bend the 4draws before sliding to the 5draw 5draw and back to the 4draw.)

Sleepy Lovers Riff

④ ④ ④ 4
③ ③ ③ 3

Good Morning Riff

① 2 ② 2 ②

Fancy Standard Blues Riff

3 ③ 4 ④ 4 ③ 4 ③ 3 3

Deep River's Bend

①

PLAYING BY YOURSELF

Harmonica is possibly the most beautiful instrument of all. It speaks of dreams, and tears, of lost friends and lovers who broke our hearts. The voice of the harmonica is what makes it so beautiful. The notes that you play are almost incidental. Let your heart speak through your harmonica. And if one day, in a bar with a sawdust floor, a slightly inebriated, curly-haired fellow gets up on the stage and starts playing some of the sweetest blues harmonica you've ever heard, ask him what key he's in and get up there and join him.

We'll have one hell of a jam.

RECORD
INDEX

RECORD INDEX

Each song in the Record Index is listed beside the key of harmonica you need to play CROSS HARP with that song. As you will notice, the first song listed in the Record Index is The Amazing Rhythm Aces' "Third Rate Romance." To accompany "Third Rate Romance," using the principles of cross harp that have been described in this book, you must play a D harp. To play cross harp with the second song, "Ella," you should play a B harp.

My method for figuring out what key of harmonica you need to play with each song was simply to put on a record, grab a harp, and wait for the music to start. Once the song in question had begun, I'd play a long 4draw. If that 4draw worked, I'd play a 3blow. If the 3blow sounded good, I'd try a couple of simple riffs. If the simple riffs seemed to fit with the music, I knew that I had the right key of harmonica harmonica.

If the 4draw clashed, or my simple riffs didn't work, then I knew that I had the wrong key of harmonica, and I tried another key of harp. On a few songs I had to try each of my twelve harps before I finally found the one that worked. The Record Index will save you this work.

Some songs have a key change. These are noted. Others, I couldn't figure out. They are indicated by a dash. You will notice that some songs require harps in the key of E flat or F sharp. Don't let this throw you. The principles of cross harp hold true no matter what key of harp you play.

Enjoy yourself.

AMAZING RHYTHM ACES

3rd Rate Romance	D	Amazing Grace	C
Ella	B	Anything	A
Railway to Heav'n	D	My Tears Flow	F
Beautiful Lie	F	Emma-Jean	G
On the Road	A	Satisfied	A
The Next Fool	A	King	A

AMERICA   HISTORY GREATEST HITS

Horse	A	Muskrat Love	A
I Need You	C	Tin Man	C
Sandman	D	Lonely People	C
Ventura	D or G	Golden Hair	A
Cross River	G	Daisy Jane	—
Your Heart	C	Woman	E

ASLEEP AT THE WHEEL   TEXAS GOLD

Ltr. J. Walker Read	D	Roll 'Em Floyd	C
Fat Boy Rag	C	The Bartender	B flat
Running After	E flat	Bump Bounce	G
Let Me Go Home	D	Where No One	B
Nothin'	F	Trouble in Mind	B flat

MOE BANDY   HERE I AM DRUNK AGAIN

Here I Am	D	Mind Your Business	A
Someone to Cheat	F	She Took More	A
What Happened	C	Oklahoma Look	F sharp
The Bottle	B flat	Let Me Go	A
Please Take Her	C	The Man You Knew	A

JACKSON BROWN   FOR EVERY MAN

Take It Easy	C	Rednecked Friend	A
Our Lady	C	The Times	B flat
Colors of the Sun	G	Ready or Not	A
I Thought	B flat	Sing My Song to Me	G
These Days	B flat	For Every Man	G

ROY BUCHANAN   SECOND ALBUM

Filthy Teddy	C	Treat Her Right	C
After Hours	C	I Won't Tell	D
Five String Blues	G	Tribute to Elmore	A
Thank You	—	She Once Lived	G

113

CROSS HARP

PAUL BUTTERFIELD   EAST MEETS WEST

Walking Blues	D	Mary Mary	D
Get Out of My Life	F	Two Trains	B flat
Gotta Mind	F	Never Say No	B flat
All These Blues	D	East West	G
Work Blues	B flat		

JOHNNY CASH   AT FOLSOM PRISON

Folsom Prison Blues	B flat	Send a Picture	—
Dark As a Dungeon	E flat	The Wall	D flat
Still Miss Someone	E flat	Egg Sucking Dog	—
Cocaine Blues	F sharp	Bathroom	B flat
25 Minutes	D flat	Jackson	F sharp
Orange Blossom	F/C	Give My Love	B flat
Long Black Veil	E flat	I Got Stripes	F sharp
		Grass of Home	F sharp
		Greystone Chapel	B flat

JESSI COLTER   JESSI

Cradle	E flat	Without You	F
One Woman Man	D	Darlin'	C
It's Morning	B flat	Would You	C
Rounder	G	All My Life	C
Here I Am	C	See Your Face	E flat

RITA COOLIDGE   THE LADY'S NOT FOR SALE

Whisky Whisky	F	My Crew	D
Everybody	E flat	Fever	D
Doughnut Man	F	In My Own Way	C
Inside of Me	E flat	I'll Be Your Baby	C
Lady's Not For Sale	C	Woman Left Lonely	A flat

JAMES COTTON   JAMES COTTON BLUES BAND

Good Time	A flat	Feeling Good	D
Lovelight	B	Sweet Sixteen	F
Something	C	Knock on Wood	A
Don't Start	D	Oh Why	E flat
Jelly	F	Blues In My Sleep	A flat
Off the Wall	A		

114

JIM CROCE   PHOTOGRAPHS & MEMORIES Greatest Hits

Bad Leroy Brown	C	I Gotta Name	A
Operator	C	In a Song	D
Photos & Memories	C	Don't Mess Around	A
Rapid Roy	A	Lover's Cross	F
Time in a Bottle	G	One Less Set	F
N.Y.'s Not My Home	D	These Dreams	G
Working	C	Roller Derby Queen	A

CROSBY, STILLS AND NASH   FIRST ALBUM

Suite Judy Blues	A	Wooden Ships	A
Marrakesh Express	C	Lady Island	—
Guinnevere	G	Helplessly Hoping	C
Don't Have To Cry	G	Long Time Gone	D
Preroad Downs	A	49 Bye Byes	E

THE CHARLIE DANIELS BAND   NIGHTRIDER

Texas	D	Funky Junky	D
Willie	G	Birmingham	A
Limestone	D	Damn Good	F
Evil	A	Tomorrow	D
All Right	G		

DOOBIE BROTHERS   STAMPEDE

Sweet Maxine	A	Take Me	D
Neal's Fandango	G	I Cheat	A
Texas Lullaby	D	Precise	—
Music Man	A	Rainy Day	G
Skat Key Soquel	—	I Been Working	A
		Double Dealing	D

DOORS   L.A. WOMAN

Riders of Storm	A
L.A. Woman	D

BOB DYLAN   BLOOD ON THE TRACKS

Tangled Up & Blue	D	Meet Me	A
Simple Twist	A	Jack of Hearts	G
You're A Big Girl	C	If You See Her	G
Idiot Wind	C	Shelter	A
Make You Lonesom'	A	Buckets of Rain	A

115

CROSS HARP

BOB DYLAN   BOB DYLAN'S GREATEST HITS

Watching the River	F	She Belongs to Me	D
Don't Think Twice	A	Watchtower	E
Lay Lady Lay	D	The Mighty Quinn	D
Stuck Inside	A	Tom Thumb's Blues	C
I'll Be Your Baby	—	A Hard Rain's	A
All I Really Want	G	If Not For You	A
My Black Pages	—	Baby Blue	A
Maggies's Farm	C	Tomorrow	—
Tonight	C	When I Paint	D
Here With You		I Shall Be Released	C
		You Ain't Going	D
		Down in the Flood	C

BOB DYLAN   DESIRE

Hurricane	—	Joey	C
Isis	E flat	Romance	G
Mozambique	G	Black Diamond	C
One More Cup	F	Sara	—
Sister	C		

EAGLES   EAGLES

Take It Easy	C	Train Leaves Here	A
Witchy Woman	C	Take the Devil	D
Chug All Night	G	Early Bird	C
Most of Us Are Sad	C	Peaceful Easy Feelin'	A
Nightingale	G	Trying	G

EAGLES   EAGLES

Doolin' Dalton	D	Fool	D
Twenty-one	D	—	C
Control	D	Outlaw	A
Tequila	C	Saturday Night	C
Desperado	C	Bitter	G
		Doolin' Dalton	D
		Desperado	D

EAGLES   ON THE BORDER

Already Gone	C	James Dean	D
You Never Cry	C	Ol' 55	F
Midnight Flyer	G	Is It True	G
My Man	B flat	Good Day in Hell	E
On the Border	A	The Best of My Love	F

FLATT AND SCRUGGS   TWENTY GREAT HITS

I Still Miss	F	Petticoat	C
99 Years	E flat	Jackson	G
When Papa Played	F	Foggy Mountain	C
John Henry	G	Kansas City	F
Cripple Creek	—	Sally Ann	C
Ballad of Jed	D	You're Gonna	C
Detroit City	G	Coal Miner's Blues	F
Soldier's Return	G	Wabash Cannonball	C
Lonesome Road	C	Memphis	B flat
Dig a Hole	F	Salty Dog	C

FLEETWOOD MAC   FLEETWOOD MAC

Monday Morning	C	Say You Love Me	D
Warm Ways	E flat	Landslide	E flat
Blue Letter	D	World Turning	G
Rhiannon	D	Sugar Daddy	D
Over My Head	G	I'm So Afraid	C

GRATEFUL DEAD   AMERICAN BEAUTY

Box of Rain	G	Ripple	D
Friend of the Devil	C	Brokedown Palace	B flat
Sugar Magnolia	D	Til the Mornin	G
Operator	B flat	Attics of My Love	D
Candy Man	C	Truckin'	A

MERLE HAGGARD   THE BEST OF THE BEST

Okie from Muskogee	A flat - A	Today I Started	C
Hungry Eyes	A flat	Mama Tried	A flat
Working Blues	D	No Reason	B flat
Farmer's Daughter	G	Every Fool	A flat
Silver Wings	A	The Fightin'	B flat
Daddy Frank	A flat		

TOM T. HALL   GREATEST HITS

Homecoming	B	Clayton Delany	F
Shoeshine Man	C	That's How I Got	A
I Miss a Lot	A	A Week	D
Switchblade	A	100 Children	E flat
I Washed My Face	F	Me and Jesus	C
Ballad of $40	G		

117

CROSS HARP

SLIM HARPO   THE BEST OF SLIM HARPO

Mohair Slim	B	Rainin'	C
Keep What I've Got	B	Shake	D
Scratch My Back	B flat	Ten-ni-nee	D
Buzz Me Baby	A	Breadmaker	A
King Bee	B flat	Tip On In	A

DAN HICKS AND HIS HOT LICKS   WHERE'S THE MONEY

Singing	C	Hook or Crook	D
Coast	B flat	Reeling' Down	F sharp
News	A	Buzzard	C
Where's the Money?	C	Traffic Jam	C
Caught	C	Home?	—
Shorty	D	Dig Deeper	—

LIGHTNIN' HOPKINS   COUNTRY BLUES

Long Time	A	Bluebird	B flat
Rainy Day	A	SeeSee Rider	B flat
Baby	B flat	Worrying	B flat
Long Gone	B flat	Til the Gin	A
Prison	E flat	Bunion Stew	—
Backwater	B flat	You Gotta	A
Gonna Pull	B flat	Go Down Old	A
		Hear My Black Dog	A

HOT TUNA   HOT TUNA

Hesitation Blues	F	Know Your Rider	D
How Long Blues	G	Oh Lord	C
Uncle Sam Blues	D	Winnin' Boy Blues	F
Don't Leave Me	C	New Song	C
Death Don't Have	A	Mann's Fate	A

WAYLON JENNINGS   THE RAMBLIN' MAN

Ramblin' Man	F	The Hunger	G
Rainy Day	D	Can't Keep My Hands	D
Cloudy Days	A	Memories of You	G
Midnight Rider	D	It'll Be Her	B
Oklahoma Sunshine	—	Amanda	D

B.B. KING   ALIVE AND WELL

So Excited	D	Key to My Kingdom	F
No Good	G	Crying Won't Help	D
Your Losin'	E flat	You're Mean	D
What Happened	A	The Thrill is Gone	E
Confessin the Blues	D		

B.B. KING   B.B. KING

No One Loves Me	D flat	Ain't Gonna Worry	E
Still My Woman	A	Chains and Things	D
Ask No Questions	D	Go Underground	D
Until I'm Dead	G	Hummingbird	B flat
King Special	D		

CAROL KING   TAPESTRY

I Feel the Earth	F	You've Got a Friend	D flat
So Far Away	G	Where You Lead	F
It's Too Late	F	Will You Love Me?	F
Home Again	D	Smack Water Jack	G
Beautiful	A flat	Tapestry	F
Way Over Yonder	F sharp	A Natural Woman	D

KRIS KRISTOPHERSON   ME AND BOBBY MCGEE

Blame It	G	Casey's Last Ride	F
To Beat the Devil	C	Nowhere	F
Me and Bobby	E	Darby's Castle	F
All Possible Words	—	For the Good	F
Help Me Make It	F	Duvalier's Dream	F
Protection	B flat	Sunday Mornin'	D

JERRY LEE LEWIS   SHE EVEN WOKE ME UP TO SAY GOODBYE

Once More	D	She Even Woke Me	G
Working Man Blues	C	Wine Me Up	C
Waiting for a Train	C	When the Grass	C
Brown Eyed Man	C	You Went Out	C
My Only Claim	F	Echoes	C
Since I Met You	G		

CROSS HARP

GORDON LIGHTFOOT   SUNDOWN

Somewhere U.S.A.	A	The Watchtowers	D
High and Dry	F sharp	Sundown	B
Seven Island Suite	E	Carefree Highway	A
Circle of Steel	B flat	The List	D
Anyone Home	—	Too Late	G

LOGGINS AND MESSINA   SITTING IN

Nobody But You	C	Back to Georgia	D
Danny's Song	G	House at Pooh	A
Vahevula	D	Listen	G
Lovin' Me	A	Same Old Wine	F
To Make a Woman	D	Rock n' Roll Mood	C
Peace of Mind	D		

JOHN LOUDERMILK   VOL. I ELLOREE

A harmonica in the Key of G will work for the entire album.

CHARLIE MCCOY   HARPIN' THE BLUES

After Hours	C	Yodel	A
Lovesick	B flat	Blues	C
Lonesome Whistle	G	St. Louis	C
Basin St. Blues	B flat	Nightlife	G
Little Walter	A	Working	E
Columbus	C		

CHARLIE McCOY   THE REAL McCOY

Today I Started	B	Lovin' Her Was Easy	D
Orange Blossom	F	Easy Lovin'	E flat
Only Daddy	A	How Can I	F
Jackson	F	Help Me Make It	A
Hangin' On	A	Country Road	F
The Real McCoy	E		

TAJ MAHAL   THE NATURAL BLUES

Good Mornin'	D	She Caught the Katy	E flat
Corinna	D	The Cuckoo	D
I Ain't Gonna		You Don't Miss	A flat
Steal My Jelly Roll	G	A Lot of Love	A
Goin' Up	E flat		
Done Changed	A		

MARIA MULDAUR   MARIA MULDAUR

Any Old Time	E flat	Walkin' One & Only	C
Midnight at Oasis	—	Long Hard Ride	F
Tenn. Mtn. Home	F	$3 Bill	E flat
Never Did Sing	G	Vaudeville Man	A
The Work Song	F	Mad Mad Me	—

JOHN MAYALL   BLUES CRUSADE

Pretty Woman	B	Driving Sideways	G
Stand Back	E	Death of J.B.	B flat
My Time	A flat	I Can't Quit You	D
Snowy Wood	A	Steamline	C
Man of Stone	E flat	Me & My Woman	F sharp
Tears In My Eyes	F	Checking My Baby	F

JOHN MAYALL   JAZZ BLUES FUSION

Country Road	E	Dry Throat	C
Mess Around	A	Exercise	F
Good Time Boogie	E flat	Got To Be This Way	E flat
Change Your Ways	A flat		

JOHN MAYALL   TURNING POINT

Laws Must Change	F	California	G
Saw Mill Gulch	A	Roxanne	F
I'm Gonna Fight	E	Room to Move	F sharp
So Hard to Share	C		

STEVE MILLER   THE JOKER

Sugar	A	Joker	—
Mary	A	Lovin'	D
Shu	A	Kitchen	E
Cash	A	Evil	D
		Believe	—

JONI MITCHELL   BLUE

All I Want	F sharp	California	A
My Old Man	D	This Flight Tonight	D flat
Little Green	E	River	C
Cary	F sharp	A Case of You	D flat
Blue	D	The Last Time	C

CROSS HARP

VAN MORRISON MOONDANCE

And It Stoned Me	C	Come Running	D
Moondance	D	Dreams of You	C
Crazy Love	D	Brand New Day	C
Caravan	C	Everyone	C
Mystic	A flat	Glad Tidings	C

VAN MORRISON TUPOLO HONEY

Wild Night	C	Tupolo Honey	B flat/E flat
Straight	A	I Wanna Roo You	A
Woodstock	A	When That Evening	D
Starting	F	Moonshine Whisky	C
You're My Woman	F		

WILLIE NELSON BEST OF WILLIE NELSON

Funny	G	Touch Me	D
Hellow Walls	F	One Step Beyond	A
The Part	E	Three Days	—
Undo the Right	—	Half a Man	C
Wake Me	G	Where My House	—
Crazy	F	Darkness	C
		Mr. Record Man	F

WILLIE NELSON REDHEADED STRANGER

Time of Preacher	A	Denver	D
I Couldn't Believe	A	Oe'r the Waves	C
Time	A	Down Yonder	C
Medley	D	Can I Sleep?	A
Blues Eyes Crying	A	Remember Me	G
Red Headed Stranger	G	Hands On	D
Time of Preacher	G	Bandera	F
Just As I Am	G		

WILLIE NELSON THE SOUND IN YOUR MIND

Sun	F	Grace	A
Time	G	Sound	F
Penny	D	Funny	G
Healing	A	Crazy	F
Thanks	D	Nightlife	F
I'd Have	A		

The harmonica on this album is all straight harp.

WILLIE NELSON   THE TROUBLE MAKER

Uncloudy Day	B flat	Garden	A
Yonder	C	Soul	B flat
Hope	D	Bye and Bye	A
Fountain	C	Gather	F
Unbroken Circle	C	Memories	A
Trouble Maker	C		

FRED NEIL   EVERYBODY'S TALKIN'

Dolphins	G	Everybody's Talkin'	G
Secret	G	Everything Happens	C
That's the Bag	C	Sweet Cocaine	F
Badi Da	G	Green Rocky Rd.	D
Faretheewell	D	Cynicraga	G

NITTY GRITTY DIRT BAND   UNCLE CHARLIE

Shelley's Blues	A	Jesse James	B
Prodigal	A	Interview	—
The Cure	D	Mr. Bojangles	B
Travelin'	A	Opus 36	—
Chicken Reel	G	Santa Rosa	A
Yukon	D	Propinquity	C
Livin'	C	Uncle Charlie	D
Clinch Mountain	D	Randy	C
Rave On	D	House at Pooh	C
Billy	G	Swannee	C *

* The key listed for Swannee is for playing straight harp.

THE OUTLAWS   WANTED

My Heroes	G	Goodhearted	G
Honky Tonk	G	Heaven or Hell	G
I'm Looking	B flat	Me and Paul	D
You Mean to Say	E flat	Yesterday's Wine	A
Suspicious Minds	G	T for Texas	C
		Another Log	D

GRAM PARSONS   SLEEPLESS NIGHTS

Heartache	A	Honky Tonks	D
Tonight	G	Together	F
Back Home	C	Honky Tonk	D
Your Angel	D	Grass	B flat
Crazy Arms	B flat	Lights	B flat
Sleepless	C	Angels	E flat

123

GRAM PARSONS   GRIEVOUS ANGEL

Return	E flat	Cash	A
Hearts	C	Hickory	D
Can't Dance	E	Love Hurts	C
Buttons	A	Las Vegas	D
Wedding	A	Hr. of Darkness	B flat

JOHN PRINE   JOHN PRINE

Illegal Smile	F	Your Flag Decal	G
Spanish Pipedream	C	Far From Me	F
Hello in There	F	Angel	C
Sam Stone	B flat	Quiet Man	D
Paradise	G	Donald and Lydia	F
Pretty Good	C	Six O'Clock News	C
		Flashback	F

PURE PRAIRIE LEAGUE   BUSTIN' OUT

Jazzman	C	Fallin'	D
Angel	G	Amie	D
My Heart	A	Boulder Skies	C
Early Mornin'	C	Amel	—
		Call Me	—

LINDA RONSTADT   PRISONER IN DISGUISE

Heat Wave	G	Love Is A Rose	F
Many Rivers	B flat	Hey Mister	G
Sweetest Gift	F	Roll Um Easy	F
Falling Down	F sharp	Tracks of My Tears	D
I Will Love You	D	Prisoner In Disguise	F
Silver Blue	E		

BOZ SCAGGS   BOZ SCAGGS

I'm Easy	B flat	Waiting for a Train	C
I'll Be Long Gone	F	Loan Me a Dime	D
Another Day	C	Sweet Release	C
Now You're Gone	—		
Finding Her	F		
Look What I Got	D		

BOB SEEGER   NIGHT MOVES

Rock and Roll	A	Sunspot	A
Night Moves	D flat	Mainstreet	A flat
The Fire	F	Come to Poppa	D
Sunburst	A	Ship of Fools	D
		Mary Lou	D

ROLLING STONES   BEGGARS BANQUET

Sympathy	A	Street Fighter	F
Station	A	Prodigal Son	A
Dear Doctor	A	Stray Cat	G
Parachute Woman	A	Factory Girl	G
Jigsaw Puzzle	A	Salt	A

ROLLING STONES   LET IT BLEED

Rambler	E	Gimmee Shelter	F sharp
Silver	B flat	Vain	E flat
Monkey Man	F sharp	Country Honk	C
What You Want	F	Live With Me	D
		Tea & Sympathy	F

ROLLING STONES   OUT OF OUR HEADS

Have Mercy	D	Satisfaction	A
Hitchhike	D	Cry to Me	D
The Last Time	D	The Undcrassistant	C
That's How Strong	E flat	Play With Fire	A
Good Times	B flat	Spider & the Fly	A
I'm Alright		One More Try	D

ROLLING STONES   STICKY FINGERS

Brown Sugar	F	Bitch	D
Sway	B flat	I Got the Blues	G
Wild Horses	C	Sister Morphine	D
Can't You Hear	G	Dead Flowers	G
You Gotta Move	F	Moonlight	G

PHOEBE SNOW   PHOEBE SNOW

Goodtimes	A	Don't Want	A
Harpo's Blues	—	Take Your Children	C
Poetry Man	G	It Must Be Sunday	D
Either or Both	E flat	No Show Tonight	F
S.F. Bay Blues	G		

CROSS HARP

BUFFALO SPRINGFIELD   AGAIN

Mr. Soul	A	Hung Upside Down	D
Child's Claim	C	Sad Memories	A
Everydays	F	Goodtime Boy	A
Expecting to Fly	E flat	Rock n' Roll	G
Bluebird	G	Broken Arrow	G

ROD STEWART   EVERY PICTURE TELLS A STORY

Every Picture	G	Maggie May	G
Seems Like a Long	F	Mandolin Wind	A
That's Alright	F	Know I'm Losing	G
Amazing Grace	A	Reason to Believe	C
Tomorrow			

STEVEN STILLS   (FIRST ALBUM)

Love the One	F	Sit Yourself Down	C
Do for Others	B flat	To a Flame	F
Church	G	Black Queen	—
Old Times	C	Cherokee	A
Go Back Home	G	We're Not Helpless	—

JAMES TAYLOR   SWEET BABY JAMES

Sweet Baby James	D	Fire and Rain	F
Lo and Behold	C	Blossom	C
Sunny Skies	F	Anywhere	C
Steamroller	C	Oh Baby Your Lip	C
Country Road	G	Suite for 20G	A
Oh Susannah	F		

TEN YEARS AFTER   A SPACE IN TIME

Days	A	Time	D
Come	D/G	Sky	D
World	A	Hard	D
Hill	A	Been	D
Baby	D	Jan	F

SONNY TERRY   BLIND SONNY TERRY

Cornbread	A	Stickhole	A
Ham	A	Rock Me	A
Lost John	A	Chain Gang Special	G
Chain Gang Blues	A	Long John	A
It Takes a Chain	A	Pick a Bale	A
Betty Dupree	A	Red River	A

CROSS HARP

BROWNIE McGEE AND SONNY TERRY

Just Rode	B flat	Po' Boy	A
Sun's Gonna Shine	A	Drinkin'	B
Brand New Car	D	Blues on Lowlands	D
Walk On	B flat		

SONNY TERRY AND BROWNIE McGEE   SONNY AND BROWNIE

People Get Ready	B flat	The Battle	G
Bring It On Home	A	Walkin'	B flat
Bring Out the Boog	C	Big Wind	B flat
Sail Away	B flat	Jesus	A
Sonny's Thing	A	God and Man	B
White Boy Lost	B flat	On the Road	A

MARSHALL TUCKER   LONG HARD RIDE

Long Hard Ride	G	Windy City Blues	D
Property Line	G	Holding On to You	G
Am I the Kind	G	You Say You Love	D
Walking the Streets	C	You Don't Live	G

JETHRO TULL   THICK AS A BRICK

B flat	B flat
	F
	B flat

JERRY JEFF WALKER   VIVA TERLINGUA

Getting By	D	Against the Wall	A
Desperados	D	Backslider	F
Sangria Wine	F	Wheel	A
Little Bird	E	London Homesick	C
Get It Out	E flat		

SONNY BOY WILLIAMSON AND THE YARDBIRDS

Bye Bye Bird	C*	Down Child	G
Pontiac Blues	C	23 Hours	F
Take It Easy	C	Out of Water	D
I Don't Care	F	Baby Don't Worry	D*
Do the Weston	C		

* Sonny Boy is playing a large, bass Marine Band Harp in this key.

CROSS HARP

SONNY BOY WILLIAMSON — BUMMER ROAD

She Got Next to Me	B flat	Lonesome Road	F
Santa Claus	D	Can't Do	D
Little Village	F	Temperature	F
		Unseen Eye	C
		Hand Out	B flat
		Open Road	E
		This Old Life	E

JESSE COLIN YOUNG — TOGETHER

Goodtimes	?	6 Days on the Rd.	E
Sweet Little Child	D	Lovely Day	F
Together	F	Creole Belle	B flat
Sweet Little 16	F	6,000 Miles	C
Peace Song	E flat	Pastures of Plenty	C

NEIL YOUNG — AFTER THE GOLD RUSH

Tell Me Why	B flat	Oh Lonesome Me	A
After the Gold Rush	G	Don't Let It	E flat
Only Love	G	Birds	E
Southern Man	G	When You Dance	E flat
Till the Morning	F	I Believe In You	B
		Cripple Creek Ferry	C

THE YOUNGBLOODS — GOOD AND DUSTY

Stagger Lee	F	Drifting	E
How Strong	D	Pontiac Blues	E flat
Willie	F	Moonshine	A
Circus	C	Circle	D
Hippie	D	Hog	D
Good and Dusty	—	Light Shine	E
Good Times	E		

Special thanks to:

Nora Nugent, who laid it out; Harry Paul, who lent me his waxer; Vissec, who edited; Tye Johnson and Toby Black, who laughed at me when I got too serious; Mrs. Thompson, who must be a lovely lady; Jeff Thelen, who made valuable suggestions; Carl and Dimi Gerle, who were very patient; G.A. and Frank Gindick, to whom the credit really belongs, Tia, who has **always** encouraged me; and lastly, *mi compadre* in all that I do, and Editor-in-chief *par excellence*, Carol Fleig.

MAKE YOUR HARMONICA A PART OF YOUR LIFE.

TWO CASSETTE LESSONS

Jon Gindick and The Cross Harp Press present two 60 minute cassette lessons based on knowledge from Jon's six years teaching beginners to play the harp. Either or both of these play-along learning experiences will enhance your fun and skill as a beginning harp player.

THE HARP PLAYER'S DREAM CASSETTE LESSON features every cross harp riff in The Natural Blues and Country Western Harmonica. It includes play-along, step-by-step instruction and slow-motion examples of the Up and Down Riff, Good Morning Riff, Traintime, tonguing, single notes, hands, bending, improvising solo and with guitar. For harmonica in the key of C. Just the thing to get beginning harp players started warbling and wailing. 60 minutes.

OL' WILLIES MELODY CASSETTE focuses on each of the 25 straight and cross harp songs notated in The Natural Blues and Country Western Harmonica. Slow-motion examples, guitar accompaniment, tips on straight harp and cross harp are included. For harp in the key of C. Play along or listen, it's a great instructional tape. 60 minutes.

Liven up your harp life with these valuable taped cassette lessons. Send for Harp Players Dream Cassette Lesson and Ol' Willies Melody Cassette Lesson today. And boogie!

HARP PLAYER'S DREAM CASSETTE LESSON . $ 6.95
OL' WILLIES MELODY CASSETTE LESSON ... $ 6.95
BOTH $11.95
THE NATURAL BLUES AND COUNTRY
WESTERN HARMONICA book .... $ 4.95
One Cassette Lesson (please specify) and Book ... $ 9.95
Two Cassette Lessons and Book $14.95

Please add 75¢ handling and postage to all orders.

All Cross Harp Press products have 15 day money back guarantee.

Send check or money order to:

> Jon Gindick
> The Cross Harp Press
> 344 Ranch Road
> Visalia, California 93277

Other Fine Books on Harmonica

Blues Harp
by Tony Glover (Oak Publications)

Blues Harp Songbook
by Tony Glover (Oak Publications)

The Harp Styles of Sonny Terry
by Sonny Terry, Kent Cooper, and Fred Palmer
(Oak Publications)

Jazz Harp
by Richard Hunter (Oak Publications)—available December
1979

☆ THE DREAM ☆

Notes

PERSISTENCE

Notes

THE REWARD